ROTOGRAPHIC
Specialist publishers of price guide reference books. Established 1959

England's Striking History.
An Introduction to the history of England and its silver Hammered coins from the Anglo-Saxons to the English Civil War.

Edited ~·, ⌐ H Perkins

1st
Re-prin¹
Revise(

ISBN: (printed version) 9⁊ₒ ⌐   ⅓5-5
eBook version © 2013, ISBN 978-0-9011/0-16-3

A wealth of information about English Coins and the monarchs and history behind them. Learn to identify hammered coins from anglo saxon times to the reign of Charles II.

Copyright Notice:

No part of this book may be reprinted or reproduced in any format, printed, electronic, now known or hereafter invented, without prior permission from Rotographic.

Errors and Omissions:

Every effort has been made to ensure that the information contained within this book is accurate and complete. However, errors do sometimes have a habit of creeping in unnoticed, and with this in mind readers are welcome to use the following email address for notifications of omissions and errors: info@rotographic.com. Readers within the UK can also call the telephone number below.

www.rotographic.com
020 308 69996

In Association with
predecimal.com

Predecimal

Contents

Introduction	4
Confusing Letters on Hammered Coins	6
Other Names on Regal Money	7
A Few words on Mint Marks	9

The Anglo-Saxon Kings of all England:

Edgar	13
Edward the Martyr	14
Aethelred II	15
Cnut	16
Harold I	18
Harthacnut	18
Edward the Confessor	19
Harold II	21

The Normans:

William I	23
William II	28
Henry I	30
Stephen	36

The Angevins:

Henry II	41
Richard I	46
John	48
Henry III	50

The Plantagenets:

Edward I	57
Edward II	63
Edward III	66
Richard II	73

The Lancastrians:

Henry IV	78
Henry V	81
Henry VI	84

The Yorkists:

Edward IV (types as Edward V)	89
Richard III	93

The Tudors:

Henry VII	95
Henry VIII	103
Edward VI	109
Mary / Philip and Mary	116
Elizabeth I	120

The Stuarts:

James I	126
Charles I	130
(The Commonwealth)	139
Charles II	140

Where do you go from here	142
An Alternative approach	144
To Clean or not to Clean	145
The Cover Images	150

Introduction

Despite the busy market in English hammered silver coins, new collectors can still buy them at remarkably low prices. You can own your first F - grade piece for less than £10, even some better grade pieces for under £25. And if you pursue your English hammered silver coin collecting to an advanced stage, many challenges and opportunities to sustain a lifetime's interest await you.

What keeps English hammered silver coins close to the top of the popularity scale among collectors, perhaps second only to Roman? A steady supply of pieces for sale at all levels of the market. Some come from old collections broken up when owners die; some from museums selling off duplicates; a lot from hoards discovered every year in ploughed fields and on building sites all over England; and large numbers as chance finds by metal detectorists whose efforts have not only added to dealers' stocks, but also brought to light several hitherto unknown or extremely rare specimens.

This small and inexpensive book cannot tell the complete story of English hammered silver coins. Nor can it, in such limited space, depict every piece. But it will introduce all the specimens any beginner or improving collector might encounter. It will certainly stimulate your appetite to learn more. And thanks to its remarkably clear illustrations it will help you to identify most of the pieces encountered in your early quests for additions to your collection.

Introduction

Keep it in your pocket and you will have no difficulty in identifying the portraits of all English monarchs, as well as the various denominations they issued, the lettering on most coins you look at closely, and the fascinating mint marks revealed by your magnifying glass. Useful sections on recommended further reading, on grading, on cleaning, as well as interesting information on monarchs and contemporary social history, will add to your growing knowledge.

We live in an age of electronic images where a camera capable of capturing six million and more pixels can be had for less than the price of many an EF grade hammered silver coin. Yet the illustrations in a lot of coin catalogues; in some hardback numismatic books; on popular internet sites such as eBay, fall short when it comes to showing clearly what a particular coin looks like in close-up. This is one area in which illustrators of an earlier age surpassed modern efforts. The images you'll find as you turn these pages originated as engravings on the pages of books published up to a couple of centuries ago. Rotographic acknowledges a debt to those artists, believing that republishing the antique illustrations alongside our updated text will encourage more newcomers to take up the coin collecting hobby. Lastly, it is important to note that the images are not shown actual sized, or to scale with each other.

ENGLANDS' STRIKING HISTORY

Confusing Letters On Hammered Coins

Your eyes will quickly adjust to reading legends. Look very closely at as many hammered silver pieces as you can get close to in dealers' trays, especially when you visit coin fairs. But, until you've gained the experience, certain letters within the legends on late Anglo-Saxon and early medieval coins can confuse the uninitiated. Those most likely to trouble the untrained eye are:

A may look like one of these:

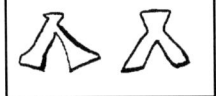

AE may look like this:

E may look like one of these:

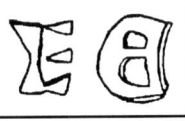

ED may look like this:

EN may look like this:

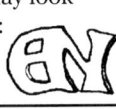

C may look like one of these:

F may look like this:

G may look like this:

H may look like these:

NG may look like this:

N may look like or of these:

O may look like this:

R may look like one of these:

TH may look like this:

U may look like this:

W may look like this:

Later medieval coinage gradually adopted the classical Roman lettering seen on our modern money.

Other Names On Regal Money

When Aedgar won the title King Of All England in 959 he began to tighten his grip on the nation's finances. On the Continent most monarchs granted the right to mint money to many subordinate lords and bishops. But Aedgar (and all those English kings and queens who followed him) took a very different view, insisting that he alone had the absolute right to issue coins. He opened dozens of mints around his kingdom where standardized silver pennies with his portrait on the obverse and the mint master's name and town on the reverse were struck in huge numbers. Even in those exceptional cases where a bishop was allowed to issue coins the mint master's name and town nevertheless appeared on at least one side.

The prominence of the moneyer's name - often in lettering as large as that used for the monarch's name - seems strange until we recall that hammered silver coins were each worth no more or less than the value of the precious metal within. That's why a pair of coin scales, and sometimes a tool to nick the edge of a coin to expose it's silver core, featured as essential kit for anyone going to a medieval market. And that's why the king insisted that the mint master must put his name and address on all work issuing from his mint. If any coin failed to pass the tests for good weight and fineness of silver everyone - from the king, the merchant, the market trader, to the humble customer - knew who to blame and where to find him.

Here's a contemporary account of what happened when Henry I learned that certain mint masters in his reign had defrauded him by issuing low-grade coins while he was abroad in France:

> *1124 AD: In this year sent the King Henry, before Christmas, from Normandy to England, and bade that mint-men in England should be mutilated in their limbs ... And the Bishop Roger of Salisbury sent over all England, and bade them that they should come to Winchester at Christmas. When they came thither, then were they taken one by one, and deprived each of the right hand and the testicles beneath. ...And that was all in perfect justice, because that they had undone all the land with great quantity of base coin...*

You might wonder why mint officials would risk their manhoods under such circumstances. Probably because the king had already cheated them by suddenly announcing the withdrawal and replacement of some older and slightly heavier pennies with new and lighter coins, leaving mint masters holding over-valued stocks of the old money. Only by skimping on silver in the new issue could they hope to recoup some of their losses.

TIP: The letter ON or OH (= OF in modern English) often appear on the reverse of early hammered silver - a clue to the place in the legend where the moneyer's name ends and the mint town's name begins.

Example: ALF ' ON STA ' = ALFWALD OF STAMFORD

A Few Words On Mint Marks

When you look at the lettering on many later medieval coins you will spot some marks that clearly do not form part of the legend; even some that are not letters at all. Most obvious are the crosses which often occur at the beginning of a legend and/or at the beginnings of words. Equally common in some reigns are apostrophe marks indicating letters omitted or elided to abbreviate the complete legend. For example: HENRICUS SEPTIMUS (= Henry VII) is sometimes abbreviated to HENRIC' SEPTIM' with the use of two elisions.

But you will also find some puzzling marks depicting birds, flowers, animals, geometric shapes, many heraldic devices, and several varieties of crescents, stars and more crosses. These are privy marks or mint marks.

A modern analogy to help appreciate the need for such marks lies in considering one of those food scares we get when something goes amiss at the supermarket and the entire nation stands in danger from a deadly bug that has found its way into a batch of canned salmon or peach melba ice-cream. In less time than it takes to contemplate the arrival of the Grim Reaper supermarket spokespersons go on-air to request that we return specific cans to the store for a full refund and perhaps a small gift to retain customer loyalty. The instant re-call system works thanks to a combination of barcodes and batch marks on every one of the tens of thousands of items on the shelves on any given day.

Later medieval mints had a similar system to protect the monarch's precious metals. These safeguards inspired faith in the silver content of

A Few Words On Mintmarks

every unclipped coin in one's purse; they even helped mint workers eager to maintain high standards when striking coins. Each die was engraved with marks that left an almost indelible record on every coin - who struck it?..with which consignment of metal?..in which year?...was the weight correct when it left the mint?...what was the condition of one or both dies at the time?...how well was the striking carried out?

You'll need a magnifying glass to spot them, but these mint marks and other privy marks and minor variations in the design on a hammered coin could identify its mint, the mintmaster, even the striker of a particular batch of coins in some cases. Look at the engraved clues to identity on the Henry VII example on the previous page - birds, crosses, keys - mint and privy marks aplenty! A fully developed system came into use in the reign of Edward III and mint marks were used on all subsequent hammered silver issuing reigns. On the next two pages you'll find illustrations depicting most of the mint marks you are likely to encounter as your collection grows.

Clipping caused damage to or even obliteration of many mintmarks positioned within the outer band of lettering where scissors were often at work. And like lettering, these raised surfaces on coins that passed from hand-to-hand over many years inevitably suffered most during the rough and tumble of circulation. They often appear worn on F-grade or lower grade coins, so to help you even further with identification, here is a listing of the main marks used in each reign.

Edward III used crosses, as did subsequent monarchs Richard II, Henry IV and Henry V. During the interrupted reign of Henry VI the lis, sun, rose and trefoil were introduced. Edward IV used them too, but he added crowns, trefoils, pansies and cinquefoils. Edward V introduced the boar's head, which was also used in the brief reign of Richard III. Five of the most interesting marks added to all that had gone before by Henry VII were a greyhound's head, an anchor, a leopard's head, an escallop and a martlet, the bird we might call a house-martin today.

Henry VIII was an enthusiastic user of mintmarks. He introduced the pomegranate, portcullis, spur, Catherine wheel and the grapple, as well as a number of letters. His son, Edward VI, added a bow, swan, ostrich head, and tun (barrel). Philip & Mary shared a mark that joined a half-rose and castle. They also used the pomegranate and lis.

A Few Words On Mintmarks

CROSSES. Many types found

LETTERS & NUMERALS

CROWNS. Frequently used

CELESTIAL BODIES
Stars, moons, suns, etc.

PLANTS & FLOWERS

ANIMALS & HUMANS

TOOLS & IMPLEMENTS
Anchors, barrels, fishhooks, wool sacks, etc.

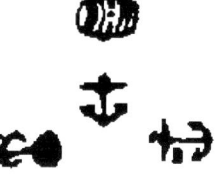

A Few Words On Mintmarks

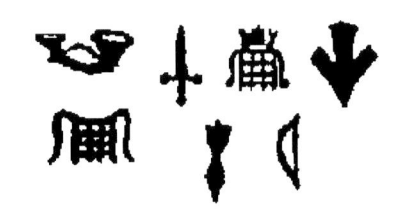

IMPLEMENTS OF WARFARE.
Including swords, spurs, castles, arrows, portcullises, halberds and more.

RELIGIOUS EMBLEMS
Croziers, bells, bibles, harps, Catherine wheels and more.

HERALDIC DEVICES

Elizabeth I used the numerals 0, 1 and 2 during the final years of her reign at the beginning of the 17th century. She also used the woolpack, key, hand, bell, and rose. James I brought the thistle mintmark from Scotland to England. He also used grapes, tower, bible and key.

When Charles I became king mintmarks were nearing the end of their run. Nevertheless Charles added a heart, plume, harp, triangle, bugle, pear, eye, and several lions and flowers to the list. During the Commonwealth only the sun and anchor were used, while Charles II naturally favoured a crown.

The Anglo-Saxon Kings Of All England

Edgar 959 - 975

Anglo-Saxon culture had flourished in Britain for more than four hundred years before Edgar took his title as *King Of The English* in 959. These islands had already witnessed four centuries of tribal warfare and threats of invasion from Scandinavia, from Viking Ireland, from Scotland, from Normandy and Saxony. But let's not forget that beyond the pages of the Anglo-Saxon Chronicles, where the wars, conquests and defeats are fully recorded, economic and social life went on often undisturbed.

Many of our 21st century cities and towns can date the foundation of their markets and churches to the Anglo-Saxon Age. And farming prospered over much of the lowland countryside. A wealth of artefacts and art confirm that merchants, priests, craftsmen and farmers led everyday lives amid the bloodshed and regal struggles. They needed coinage for day-to-day transactions as much as kings needed coinage to pay their armies, to secure the services of mercenaries, to bribe their enemies and to pay for luxury goods.

Anglo-Saxon Kings - Edgar, Edward the Martyr

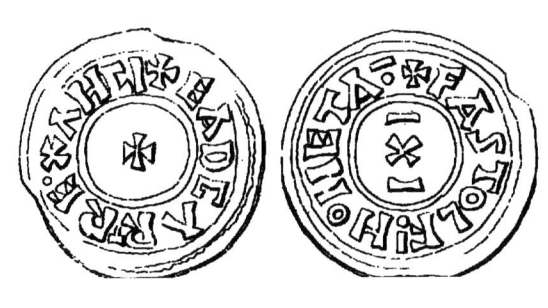

Edgar, as the second son of Edmund, King of Wessex, Kent, West Mercia and East Anglia, only gained a throne after his elder brother, Eadwig All-Fair, proved a poor ruler who often quarrelled with bishops, lords and in-laws. They forced Eadwig to cede half the kingdom, including recently acquired Northumbria and Mercia, to his brother even though young Edgar had barely reached the age of twelve in 957. Two years later Eadwig died, leaving Edgar as sole king of the whole of England.

The Anglo-Saxon Chronicles record that he gave generously to monasteries; ravaged Thanet to quell a revolt; took three wives; kept a squad of Viking mercenaries as his household guards; and - in 973 - introduced new silver pennies for the whole of England. As shown on the previous page, the design had the king's portrait and name on the obverse, with a central cross and the moneyer's name and town on the reverse. The coin above is an earlier issue with no portrait.

Edward the Martyr: 975-978

Edgar's eldest son, Edward, reigned for barely three years before an assassin murdered him at Corfe Castle, Dorset. His silver pennies followed the design introduced by his father, Edgar.

**Lettering clues to identity.
Look for:**

EADPEARD REX

Aethelred II (The Unready): 978-1016

This longest-serving Anglo-Saxon king of all-England was a lad of twelve when he inherited the throne following the bloody murder of his brother. Initially affairs of state were left to his counsellor, the Bishop of Winchester; but when the bishop died in 984 Aethelred ruled wisely for several years, strengthening the economy before he raised taxes to maintain his ever-growing army.

In the 990's successive waves of Viking raiders threatened to invade Eastern England and overwhelm the English army—until Aethelred had what he considered a sudden inspiration: to use his coffers of silver tax coins to pay off any Viking captains who agreed to sail their ships back to Scandinavia. Many took up the offer and Aethelred stumped up more than £100,000 (millions in modern terms), which explains why so many English coins of his reign are found today in hoards located by Scandinavian metal detectorists.

Aethelred's thirty-eight-year reign provided collectors with a number of bust variations including right and left-facing heads.

It became clear after the year 1000 that *Danegelt* payments attracted more Vikings than they deterred. Aethelred changed tactics and announced an ethnic cleansing policy: all Scandinavians who had settled in England must die. Unfortunately one of the first victims was the sister of Swein Forkbeard (also known as Sweyn, Sven, Svein or Svend), king of Denmark, who at once declared war on England and sent many more longships.

Another change of tactics by Aethelred in 1012 saw the appointment of a former Viking - Thorkel the Tall - as commander of an enlarged English navy. After many sea and land battles Swein Forkbeard died of old age in 1014. Alas, Aethelred's troubles with invaders continued when the new Danish king - Cnut - took up the struggle where his father had left off. When Aethelred died in 1016 Cnut sent a huge fleet sailing towards England.

Aethelred's reign introduced several innovations on coin reverses, including long and short-cross designs and pictorial elements. See above left and right.

Lettering clues to identity. Look for: AEDELRED

Cnut: 1016-1035

When Forkbeard died, his son Cnut swore to take the English crown by defeating Aethelred. But the English king died in bed before they met.

Aethelred's son, Edmund Ironside, who issued no coins, was betrayed by the Earl of Mercia and lost his first battle against Cnut. Edmund sued for peace, surrendered half the kingdom to the Dane, then died within a month, leaving Cnut to take the crown. The new king promptly married Aethelred's widow to secure his hold on the kingdom.

During the next few years he purged his court of many English nobles and gave generous earldoms to the few he trusted. He also kept a large regiment of *huscarls* - Scandinavian mercenaries - as his royal bodyguard. With no Danegelt payments to find in taxes, the English economy prospered. Cnut opened several new mints across the country and the number of silver pennies in circulation greatly increased.

Anglo-Saxon Kings - Cnut

When his brother, the king of Denmark, died in 1018 Cnut became the ruler of an empire that included England, Denmark and parts of Sweden and Norway. English silver pennies seem to have circulated throughout Cnut's realms; indeed some English moneyers had mints in Denmark. But no major innovations in designs occurred. Almost all silver pennies kept to the styles of previous reigns with the monarch's head and title on the obverse, and a cross plus the moneyer's name and location on the reverse.

Lettering clues to identity. Look for CNVT

Some of Cnut's silver pennies.

Harold I 1035-1040

Cnut died aged 39, leaving sons by different wives to quarrel over the crown. Harold Harefoot had the support of most northern nobles, but no southern bishop would crown him until he offered the south of the kingdom to his half-brother, Harthacnut, who now ruled in Denmark. A war in Norway kept the Dane too busy to come to England, so Harold annexed the south in 1038. When the war in Norway was won in 1039, Harthacnut set sail for England with a fleet of sixty ships. Bad weather kept the fleet on the coast of Flanders until 1040, by which time Harold was dead and buried. But when Harthacnut eventually landed he ordered Harold's body to be dug up and thrown into a swamp.

Lettering clues to identity. Look for: HAREI; HAROLD; HARALD

Harthacnut: 1035- 1042

Harthacnut built another large war fleet, determined to hold his new kingdom. But the taxes he imposed brought him few friends. Harthacnut had no children, so when Edward, the surviving son of Aethelred II and Emma of Normandy, arrived in England with the backing of the powerful Duke of Normandy, Harthacnut offered him joint rule and succession.

During Harthacnut's reign large numbers of Danish coins flowed into England, but his English silver pennies kept to the standard style.

**Lettering clues to identity. Look for:
HARDACNVT; HARDECNVT**

Edward the Confessor 1042 - 1066:

The term *Confessor* is applied to him by historians simply to distinguish between this monarch and the earlier Edward murdered in Corfe Castle and afterwards sometimes referred to as Edward the Martyr. In fact the later Edward might best be remembered as Edward the Undecided because he seemed unable to make up his mind about a successor - a situation that had the most disastrous consequences for Anglo-Saxon monarchy and society.

He had a strong claim to England's throne as the son of Aethelred II and Queen Emma. He also had the firm backing of his cousin, William of Normandy; and when he married Edith, daughter of Earl Godwine the future looked bright. But in 1051, after ten years of marriage, no heir had been sired. The king blamed his wife, packed her off to a nunnery and looked to Normandy for a new bride. In response Godwine and his son, Harold, Earl of East Anglia, took most of the English fleet to sea and began attacks on coastal towns in the south and west. Edward capitulated and gave up his plans to remarry. He may have promised the crown to the Godwine family at that time.

Anglo-Saxon Kings - Edward the Confessor

But when Edward lay childless on his deathbed in 1066, William of Normandy claimed that he had been promised England's crown for his support of Edward in 1042. The scene was set for calamity.

Politically inept perhaps, but Edward left rich pickings for coin collectors. His regal portrait appears left-face, right-face, front-face, even seated, on his silver pennies, which vary quite considerably in size and weight, though all were indeed pennies. Many hoards of Edward the Confessor coins have included pennies that had been sheared at the mint into halves and quarters as a means of minting halfpence and farthings. (Shearing is quite different from cutting circulated coins.)
Lettering clues to identity. Look for: EADPARD ... EDPARD ... EDPD ... EDPER

Some of Edward the Confessor's coins.

Harold II: 1066

His troubles began in 1064 when Earl Tostig of Northumbria was outlawed for misrule by Edward the Confessor. Tostig fled to Norway where he urged king Harald Hardraada to challenge for the crown of England when Edward died. Hardraada invaded in 1066, defeating a northern army and sacking York. Harold, newly crowned and awaiting an invasion by William of Normandy, led his army on a forced march to Stamford Bridge, a few miles from York, where he surprised Hardraada and annihilated his army.

Then came news that William had landed at Pevensey. Harold's tired force hurried south to meet the Normans at the village now known as Battle, near Hastings. Harold almost pulled off a second victory; but a Norman arrow brought him down. The reign of Anglo-Saxon kings was at an end.

Lettering clues to identity. Look for: HAROLD
Two coins of Harold II

The Normans
1066 - 1154

The Normans proudly traced their ancestry to a Viking sea-captain named Rollo who marauded along the coast of what we now call France in the late 9th century. He sailed his longships up the River Seine and built a stronghold at Rouen. By 924 his territory had expanded to include much of north-west France. The king of Francia granted Rollo the title Duke of Normandy in return for his military services as a buffer between Francia and fresh waves of Vikings sweeping down the North Sea from Scandinavia.

Rollo soon revealed a talent for administration to match his superlative skills as a warrior. He also embraced Christianity, though on his death bed he made a blood sacrifice to Odin as well as a generous gift to the Church. And he encouraged his Vikings to take Frankish wives and learn the local French dialect. As the lands bordering Normandy fragmented into a group of quarrelling feudal territories Rollo and his successors ensured by diplomacy and sword that the Duchy of Normandy grew richer, stronger and greedy for wider borders. But even Rollo would surely have expressed mild surprise to learn that his great-great-great-grandson had been crowned king of England, and that Viking blood would course through the veins of English royalty for centuries to come.

William I : 1066-1087

The illegitimate son of Robert the Magnificent and Herleva, the daughter of a tanner, William was the only male offspring his father had to choose from when he named his successor in the event of unexpected death while on a pilgrimage to Jerusalem. In fact the Duke succumbed to disease on the journey and William became Duke of Normandy at the tender age of eight. He survived a dangerous childhood during which his mother married a nobleman and bore him two sons - Odo and Robert - who might have challenged William for the ducal coronet. But the young William found favour with his overlord, the French king, and held onto his title precariously into his late teens when he began to exhibit his remarkable skills at warfare.

Aged 19 he led his army against a challenge for Normandy by the Count of Brionne; then an even greater challenge a couple of years later by the Count of Anjou, who also suffered defeat. William's diplomatic skills led him to a marriage with the daughter of the Count of Flanders, a powerful ally who aided William when the King of France attacked Normandy on learning that William had been promised the crown of England by Edward the Confessor. All threats to Normandy's borders were repulsed and the uneasy peace gave William the opportunity he had been waiting for - to claim the English throne in 1066.

The Normans - William I

As every schoolboy knows, the Normans won at Hastings. William made sure that his half-brothers, Odo and Robert, gained huge estates in England. They and his battle-hardened troops subjected England, Wales, lowland Scotland and much of Ireland to Norman rule and laws, though William spent most of his reign in Normandy, fighting till his death against threats to his borders.

England's monetary system was one of the few Anglo-Saxon institutions that altered little when the Normans rolled in, though William I issued huge numbers of silver pennies and operated more than seventy mints as the coins of former Anglo-Saxon monarchs poured into the melting pot to emerge from the striker's anvil bearing the new king's portrait. Nevertheless the basic design elements - regal bust and ruler's name on the obverse; moneyer's name, location of mint, plus a cross on the reverse- remained the same. Glance at these examples of early Norman pennies and we will explain how to put William I's coins into ordered groupings on the next page. ...

Lettering clues to identity. Look for: PILLEMUS ... PILLEM ... PILLELM

The Normans - William I

The Normans - William I

An immediate difficulty arises when trying to identify William I coins from their obverse legends alone: the heir, William II, used the same spellings on his coins. However, there is one group we can positively identify as belonging to the father. They have the word PAXS (=PEACE) on the reverse. You will find one letter within an annulet (circle) in each of the four quadrants of the cross ...

Thus:

A combination of those letters on a reverse, and **PILLEMUS ... PILLEM ... PILLELM** on the obverse clinches the coin as an issue of William I. Note however that the PAXS referred to is not that immediately following 1066, but the hard-won peace achieved in 1086-87 with his own disgruntled Norman barons.

A second clearly defined and easily spotted group has a left-facing profile. The succeeding monarch issued no left profile coins, so we can confidently assign this group to William I

On a third group of coins the king is flanked by two sceptres, thus:

This pose was never used by his heir, so this group also belongs to William I.

A fourth group depicts the king with a star to left and right of his bust. Unfortunately William II also used two stars in this manner. But if the reverse has a square at centre with curving sides as shown to the right it's a William I issue.

The Normans - William I

A fifth group depicts the king beneath a canopy supported by two columns, thus:

When looking at a worn coin confusion may arise between the columns of the canopy and the flanking sceptres already mentioned. In such a case examine the reverse. The canopied coin should have what advanced numismatic works describe as *a double quadrilateral with sides curved inwards, an annulet at its centre, and fleurs at the angles*. Something like the small image to the left.

It becomes possible at an advanced stage in one's collecting to identify other groups and positively assign them to William I or William II. At this stage you should learn to spot the five types covered here and regard yourself as a fairly knowledgeable beginner. You might also go down a collecting route followed by many before you and train your eye to spot the names of some of the mints used by the Normans. Pennies of this era at the lower end of the price scale probably came from a mint that struck large numbers of coins, or one that struck coins which ended up in a Norman hoard. Several have come to light in recent years. Shown below are the commoner spellings of busy Norman mints:

London:	LVNDN ... LVNDNE ... LVNDENI .. LUN ... LUNI ... LI .. LVI ... LOUN
Canterbury:	CATPAI ... C ... CNT ... CANTO .. EANT, CNTLI
Dover:	DUF ... DOFR ... DOI ... DOVOR
Ipswich:	GIP ... GIPE ... GIPSP
Lincoln:	LINCOLNE ... LINC ... LINI
Oxford:	OXSN ... OXNE ... OXNEF ... OXSI OXI
Stamford:	STN ... STI

Bear in mind that illiteracy carried no stigma in those days. The king could barely read or write Norman French, and he gave up his attempts to learn English after his first few lessons. Blundered engraving of coin dies must therefore by regarded as by no means unusual. Standards in minting declined rapidly in subsequent years, but even in William I's reign many coins carried lettering errors. Add the widespread practice of clipping, and the commonplace method of making halfpence and farthings by shearing or cutting whole coins, and it's hardly surprising that most collectors come across examples of Norman coinage they cannot accurately ascribe to a particular monarch or a known mint.

William II: 1087-1100

When William the Conqueror lay on his deathbed he gave Normandy to his eldest son, Robert; he gave £5,000 to his second son, Henry; and he gave England to his third son, William, known as William Rufus to historians because of his ginger hair. Despite appearances of his coins, in real life William II was short and fat. Various ecclesiastical writers accused him of licentiousness, dandyism, even homosexuality, though other sources claimed the accusations stemmed from his habit of taxing the Church heavily whenever he needed money for his various wars. But he proved a strong ruler, putting down at least two revolts by his barons; campaigning successfully in Scotland and Wales; invading Normandy twice in attempts to wrest it from his brother. He also found time to supervise the building of Carlisle Castle, the White Tower of London, and Westminster Hall. He eventually became ruler of Normandy when Robert mortgaged his lands to William when raising funds for a crusade to Jerusalem.

The circumstances surrounding his death at the age of forty in a New Forest hunting accident have always aroused suspicion, given that his younger brother, Henry, witnessed the incident, then at once sped off for Winchester where he seized the royal coffers, thence to Westminster and coronation three days later.

William II allowed England's coinage to deteriorate to a sorry state. Some mints closed; others struck pennies using worn and faulty dies; still more cheated by issuing underweight money or adding base metal to the silver. Significantly in the examples shown above, the first has been quite deeply nicked by someone who doubted its intrinsic silver value.

Henry I: 1100-1135

Following his coronation three days after the death of William Rufus, Henry sought to legitimize his English kingship by marrying the sister of Edgar, the nobleman briefly proclaimed king of the Anglo-Saxons after Harold's death at Hastings thirty-four years earlier. But when Robert of Normandy returned from his crusade he claimed England's throne and landed with substantial forces, only to retreat rather than face the larger army Henry had gathered to oppose him. A few years later Henry turned the tables and invaded Normandy. Robert was captured and taken to Cardiff castle where he later died. Henry now ruled on both sides of the Channel, though the close kin of Robert constantly sniped at his borders.

The Normans - Henry I

By 1120 all seemed settled so far as the next succession went - until disaster struck when the famous White Ship sank in the mouth of the Seine with half the Anglo-Norman aristocracy aboard. One of the passengers was Henry's only son. A hurried marriage with the daughter of his ally the Count of Louvain took place, but after four year Henry still had no son. In desperation he recalled to Normandy his only surviving child, his twenty-five-year-old daughter Matilda, widow of the Emperor Henry V, and arranged her marriage to the fourteen-year-old son of the Duke of Anjou, another ally. He then made his remaining barons in England swear to accept Matilda as his successor. They obliged; but on Henry I's death in 1135, his nephew Stephen crossed the Channel and seized the throne in much the way Henry had grabbed it thirty-five years earlier.

We have already mentioned Henry's savage treatment of moneyers found guilty in 1124 of coining underweight coins. Weights may have improved when the new men still endowed with right hands and testicles took over; but the dies they used were often badly worn. As a result coins in better than f-grade rarely appear in dealers' lists, or as detectorists' finds.

Advanced collectors divide Henry I coins into a daunting fifteen categories. Have a look at the illustrations below and we will show you how to spot coins from some of the groups on the next page ...

Lettering clues to identity. Look for: HENRI ... HENRICUS ... HENRY ... HENRIC ... HENR ..

ENGLANDS' STRIKING HISTORY

The Normans - Henry I

Worn coins, old dies, poor workmanship, low-grade silver, clipping, cutting to make halfpence and farthings - all militate against accurate identification of Henry I pennies. However, if you keep in mind the obverse lettering clues provided and use that information with these additional pointers, you should be able to identify and date the following types:

The Normans - Henry I

Henry issued PAX coins in 1103-1104 commemorating a peace treaty with brother Robert. Look for PAX on the reverse, as at left here.

Four or five left-facing portraits were issued during the reign, but only one had a reverse as shown to the right - a cross fleury with an annulet at centre - dating it to 1102-1103.

If you spot a Henry I obverse as shown here with annulets on each side of the portrait, it dates from 1101-1102.

A star close to the king's bust alerts you to a coin minted 1105-1106; but check the reverse, which must have a voided cross with fleurs in angles as shown at left.

ENGLANDS' STRIKING HISTORY

The Normans - Henry I

Three stars to right of the bust, as shown to the left, are seen on coins dated 1106-1107. If worn, check the reverse for crosses.

Another left-facing profile is shown to the right. If the reverse has a cross with annulets in its angles, the penny dates from 1109-1110.

Here's a crude front-facing bust which might seem difficult to date; but if the reverse has five annulets as shown above, the coin dates from 1104-1105.

Look for a cluster of four annulets to right of Henry's bust, as shown here. If the reverse shows four more annulet clusters around a central cross, the penny dates from 1107-1108.

ENGLANDS' STRIKING HISTORY

The Normans - Henry I

This coin with a left facing bust can be dated by its reverse which has a star within a lozenge at its centre. It dates from 1120-1122.

This left-facing bust can be accurately dated by a reverse with two circles of lettering to 1110-1114.

You can now identify 10 groups of Henry I coins, which is probably better than some experienced collectors!

Stephen: 1135-1154

As the son of William I's daughter, and as no more than a nephew of Henry I, Stephen had only a weak claim to the English throne. His mother sent him to the English court as a child where he became a favourite of king Henry, who gave him substantial estates on both sides of the Channel. Stephen's brother, Robert, who also came to England for his education, took to the Church and rose to become Bishop of Winchester in 1129.

Stephen was in Normandy when Henry I died. He at once rushed to England where his brother helped him to seize the royal treasury at Winchester and then to persuade the Archbishop of Canterbury to crown Stephen as king. All those involved in this coup ignored their sworn promise to the old king that they would accept Henry's only child and daughter, Empress Matilda of Germany, as the rightful heir. She at once attacked Stephen's lands in Normandy, and by 1139 the empress had sufficient support from barons in the west to carry the struggle to England. All-out civil war ensued from power bases in London, where Stephen had most support, and from Bristol and the south-west, where Matilda held sway.

With a lack of regal authority in the west, on the Scottish border, and across the Channel, the king's coinage inevitably deteriorated. Study these examples, they will be discussed on the next page:

The flans on which these coins were struck vary in size, and most are crudely shaped. Nevertheless, all were issued as pennies. The next thing to note is the wide variety in portraits. Despite Stephen's hold on the London mint, numerous pieces were struck for him in the south-eastern provinces where coining techniques were cruder than in the capital. We can also see much variety in the crowns worn on the royal head. Indeed, the only obverse feature we can reliably use to identify his coins is Stephen's name. Although the moneyers had idiosyncratic spelling rules, their rendering of the king's name is as least recognizable to the modern eye. On the coins it comes out as:

STIEFN ... STIEFNE ... STIFN ...
STEF ... STE ... STIEN ... STEPHANUS

Sometimes the 'N' is reversed; frequently letters are missing as a result of wear or poor striking; but if you can see any of those groups of letters you probably have a silver penny of Stephen in your hand. Here is the only exception:

This coin has the letters PERERIC ... sometimes **PERERICM**. Numismatists now think that some moneyers of the period living in areas that might have changed hands or allegiance during the war used these letters to make the coins acceptable to both parties, claiming they had inadvertently spelled the previous monarch's name - HENRICUS - incorrectly.

Advanced collectors look to the reverses of Stephen's coins in attempts to determine where they were minted. On the reverse of the PERERIC example to the right the letters **ON (= of)** are very clear. The letters following **ON** will always be the mint town, usually abbreviated and often misspelled. (In this example the letters **LU** abbreviate the more usual **LUND** for London. But with more than seventy mints in operation during the reign identifying a mint is often less straightforward. **LU(ND) ... BED ... BRIST ... CANT ... DOFVER ... GLO ... HEREFO ... LINCOL ... OXEN** ... we can all make reasonable guesses at (London, Bedford, Bristol, Canterbury, Dover, Gloucester, Hereford, Lincoln, Oxford). But what about **EVER ... PIREC ... PAR ... SCIEFT ... NORPT ... RIS ... ?** (York, Worcester, Warwick, Shaftesbury, Norwich, Castle Rising)

Ironically, the issue most advanced collectors seek, in f-grade if possible, in this reign is the WATFORD - not a mint town, but a spot where a large hoard of Stephen coins came to light. Their most recognizable feature after the monarch's name is the *cross moline* as depicted on the reverse of the PERERIC example above. The other commonly encountered crosses - *plain cross, voided cross and cross fleury* – are seen on the reverses shown on the previous page.

The Normans - Stephen

The coins above were issued by two of Stephens supporters - his brother Henry as the Bishop of Winchester. (Note the crozier and the EPC abbreviation of the Latin word for Bishop.) The horseman on the right is Robert, Earl of Gloucester. He supported Stephen initially, but later switched allegiance, only to be captured and ransomed for the king a couple of years later. Although rare, these local issues are occasionally found by metal detectorists.

Matilda may have had a stronger legal claim to the English throne, but her coins, all struck at provincial mints with worn or crudely made dies, survive in even poorer grades than Stephen's money. The two examples shown below have only the letter M as a clue to their issuer.

As the war dragged on, the fortunes of both sides changed dramatically. In the early stages Stephen might have swept Matilda and her supporters into the Bristol channel, but a series of blunders   allowed the empress to gain the upper hand. In 1141 while besieging Norwich castle the king was captured and taken as a prisoner to Bristol. But a few months later the king's forces captured the Earl of Gloucester. An exchange of these two illustrious hostages restored the status quo.
During the 1150s Matilda gained many victories and eventually entered London, only to suffer ignominious rejection by its citizens.

The Normans - Stephen

Further twists and turns in the plot included Matilda's escape from a besieged castle; the loss of Normandy by Stephen, and his failed attempts to have his son, Eustace, declared heir to the English throne. Eventually the two contenders were forced by their barons to sign the Treaty of Winchester. Under its terms Stephen was to rule as King of England in his lifetime; Matilda's son, Henry, would then take the crown.

Here are examples of other provincial and unofficial coins issued during the civil war. They include pieces by Eustace (the top two coins) and William, both sons of Stephen. The coin at bottom right may depict Stephen and Matilda and commemorate the Treaty of Winchester, though some authorities say the figure on the right is Stephen's wife, who was also called Matilda.

The Angevins: 1154-1272

Today the name *Anjou* conjures aromas and tastes of delicious rosé wines. But among historians the same word powerfully associates with the murder of Archbishop Thomas à Becket by Henry II's knights; with the crusades of Richard the Lionheart; with the Runnymede signing of Magna Carta by King John. All three events, not to mention the loss of most French possessions and the annexing of the whole of Ireland, took place during the tumultuous dynasty of the Angevins, whose ancestors were the counts of Anjou. At the height of their powers an Angevin ruled Normandy, Aquitaine, Maine, Touraine, Poitou, England and Ireland. Nevertheless, their loyalty and cultural identification with Anjou remained so strong that none of the English kings of this royal line - Henry II, Richard I, John or Henry III thought of himself as anything but Angevin.

Henry II: 1154- 1189

The tasks facing Henry II, son of a Norman mother, but grandson of a count of Anjou, when he came to the English throne might have daunted a weaker man. But Henry vowed that on his accession he would restore the kingdom to the peace and prosperity formerly enjoyed in the reign of Henry I. The economy lay in utter ruins after almost twenty years of civil war, so the king appointed some of the best men in the kingdom to overhaul and reorganize the Exchequer to ensure enough taxes were

The Angevins - Henry II

gathered to pay for programmes such as strengthening the country's northern border with new and repaired castles, as well as demolishing many of the unauthorized castles built by the barons during the civil war.

For the first four years of his reign Henry could do little about the bad money from the previous reign that continued to circulate. But in 1158 he acted as Henry I had done and called every moneyer in England to account. They fared better than the unfortunates of 1124, losing their livelihoods rather than their testicles. With trusted mint masters appointed to thirty-one mints, Henry now ordered the total withdrawal of the old money and its replacement by newly designed coins with reverses as shown on the previous page. Numismatists called them *cross-and-crosslets pennies*; but the name *Tealby pennies* is also often heard, thanks to the discovery of a substantial hoard of more than 5,000 cross-and-crosslet pennies at Tealby, Lincs in 1807.

Due in part to the shortage of experienced mint craftsmen, and to the scale of the operation, the cross-and-crosslet issues included many poorly struck pieces on roughly cut flans; but the coins gained widespread acceptance because they were made from fine silver of good weight and they bore the king's name. They are popular among today's collectors who group them into six classes distinguished in part by hair, or lack of it, on the monarch's portrait.

This can prove difficult for a beginner faced with coins showing centuries of wear. It's easier to look for a front-facing bust, crowned and holding a sceptre in his right hand, as at left, where the hairless class is shown. Beginners should next closely examine the obverse lettering. If some or all of it is legible these Tealby issues can be dated fairly accurately.

The Angevins - Henry II

HENRI REX ANG is seen on the Class A hairless bust. (See illustration on Henry II Introduction.) These coins date from 1158-1161 approx.

HENRY REX AN is seen on Class B coins which also have a hairless bust, with minor differences in the lines suggesting garments. They date from 1161-1165 approx.

HENRI R ANG is seen on Class C coins which depict a single curl of hair on the monarch's head. A decorated collar is also shown. As with Class B, these coins date from 1161-1165 approx.

HENRI REX is seen on Class D coins which are very similar to Class C in appearance, with minor differences on the garments. They date from 1165-1168 approx.

HENRI REX A is seen on Class E coins, which are similar to Class D in appearance, with minor differences on the garments. They date from 1168-1170 approx.

HENRI REX is seen on Class F coins. Although the legend is identical to Class D, this class shows the bust with a bunch of curls. The coins date from 1170-1180.

Reverse styles on all six classes did not alter at all. Each coin has the cross-and-crosslets surrounded by lettering. If unworn, look for another small cross within the lettering. This indicates that the next letter begins the moneyer's name, probably abbreviated. Then comes **ON (= OF)** followed by the mint town, again very often shortened. Specialist collectors will know all moneyers' names and the years in which the different mints operated. Beginners will probably satisfy their curiosity if they can identify the mint town. Bear in mind that 31 took part in production of the Tealby pennies, and that blundered lettering and wear militate against recognizing all names. Towns most often encountered include:

S.EDM (Bury St Edmunds) ... **CANTO** (Canterbury) ... **CARDU** (Cardiff) ... **GIPES** (Ipswich) ... **LINC** (Lincoln) ... **LUND** (London) ... **NORED** (Norwich) ... **TED** (Thetford)

SHORT CROSS COINAGE

In 1180 Henry tackled the unresolved problem of quality control in his mints, first by reducing their number to eleven, then by paying for the services of a skilled mint master from Tours - Philip Aymary - to make the dies and to superintend the introduction of entirely new coins struck on flans of uniform size. Displaying none of the ostentation one might have expected from a powerful and confident ruler, Henry kept the designs on his new money very simple: a full-face portrait, his mitre in right hand, his name in Latin **(HENRICUS REX)** around the perimeter of the obverse; and on the reverse a small voided (open) cross with four pellets in each quarter and the usual moneyer's name and town around it.

The voided cross proved a clever innovation. It allowed merchants and traders to cut the new pennies accurately into halfpence and farthings. So long as the customer could see one bar of the cross along the cut edge he/she could be certain the coin had been fairly divided.

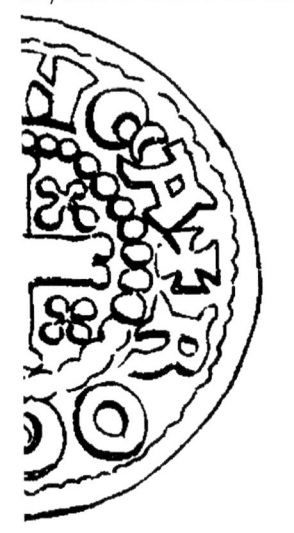

A halfpenny cleanly cut to leave one bar clearly visible on the horizontal of the cross.

The Angevins - Henry II

No bigger than the nail on a little finger, this cut farthing was valued as small change.

To say that the new money proved popular considerably understates matters. His subjects liked the coins so much the king broke with long tradition and scarcely altered the design during the remaining nine years of his reign. For today's collectors the results amount to much complexity because Henry's sons and grandson - Richard I, John and Henry III - also kept the design almost unchanged. They even remained loyal to the lettering on the obverse. **HENRICUS REX** was the name those kings placed on their English coins, claiming that it gave a sense of continuity to the House of Angevin. So short cross pennies eventually spanned sixty-seven years and four reigns unchanged in all but the most minute of detail!

The devil is in that detail. Many experienced collectors have a hard time deciding which monarch's penny they hold in their hand when it's a short cross type. They must consider mint towns, portraits, lettering styles; and often closely compare one king's penny with another's before reaching a firm decision. In time I hope every reader of this little book will progress to that level of expertise. As a start I urge you to learn to pick out one or two short cross pieces from each reign and assign them with some certainty to one of the four monarchs under discussion.

ENGLANDS' STRIKING HISTORY

Let's begin with the king who introduced short-cross pennies If, when examining a coin, you see lettering like the coin shown at the bottom of the previous page, in which the letters **E** and **C**, (highlighted) have blocky and angular shapes, then it's very likely to be a coin of Henry II because none of the other Angevins used that style. Alas, not all of Henry II's pennies use these squared letters; but at least you have made a start on recognizing some money from his reign.

As part of his expansionist plans, Henry II married Eleanor of Aquitaine who bore him four ambitious sons, each promised a fair share of the inheritance by their father. But the untimely deaths of two sons, and the fact that Henry lived long enough to see the remaining two grow to manhood and rivalry, sowed the seeds of doom for the dynasty.

Richard I: 1189-1199

The popularity of this king's coins among collectors owes much to his Hollywood image as *Richard the Lionheart*. In fact the only coins that bear his name were issued on the Continent where he spent most of his life despite holding the crown of England for ten years.

His apprenticeship as a medieval ruler began at fourteen when his father ceded control of Aquitaine, hoping the responsibilities would curb the lad's wild spirits. Instead, at sixteen Richard began conquering new lands on Aquitaine's borders; and by his early twenties his renown as a skilled military tactician had spread throughout Christendom.

The Angevins - Richard I

To his fathers great annoyance Richard became the first northern prince to pledge his sword to the Holy Land crusade after Jerusalem fell to the Muslims under Saladin in 1187. But the death of Henry I and a coronation kept him away from the battlegrounds until 1190, by which time he had arranged for his wife to rule in England during his absence. In Palestine he fought alongside the king of France for a year. They drove Saladin's armies from half the Holy Land and were set to lay siege to Jerusalem when the French king suddenly announced his departure for home. Richard's army fought alone for several months. Meanwhile, back in Europe, the French king overran Richard's lands and plotted to have him killed during his homeward journey.

RICARDUS is not found on Richard's English pennies. This is a Continental issue.

In fact, Richard was taken prisoner and handed over to the German emperor, who demanded a ransom equal to four years' royal taxes in England. To make matters worse, Richard's younger brother, John, spread a rumour that the king had died. However, his attempts to seize the English throne were thwarted by the queen, who eventually raised the ransom money. Freed at last in 1194, Richard made only a fleeting visit to England before setting off to regain his lost lands on the Continent. He battled for five years, taking back all of the old Angevin empire, and he was at the gates of Paris when a crossbow bolt felled him.

The Angevins - Richard I, John

RICHARD I's SHORT CROSS COINAGE.

As explained earlier, you will find no square E or C on Richard's pennies; but the same applies to those of John and Henry III. However, there is a feature on two of the four classes within Richard's reign that marks them out: on two of the portraits the king appears to have a stubble chin rather than a beard because the beard's hairs are represented by pellets and not by curls. So half of Richard's pennies can be identified as follows:

If you see stubble on the chin it's probably a coin of Richard the Lionheart

John: 1199-1216

Most of us learned from junior school history books that this king signed Magna Carta at Runnymead; that he lost a fortune in gold and silver while attempting to ford The Wash; that he was a thoroughly bad monarch England did not deserve. Here are some new facts that might marginally modify your opinion:

As the youngest son of the family, John received no lands when his father, Henry II, divided up the Angevin empire. He had to live with the soubriquet *John Lackland* for years afterwards. And when his brother, Richard I, inherited the empire he, too, gave none of the rich Continental domains to his brother. Two years into his reign Richard even nominated a favourite nephew as his heir, offering his younger brother little more than the lordship of Ireland, where the young prince John issued his own coins, two of which are shown below:

The Angevins - John

So it's hardly surprising that John, who was in France when news came of Richard's death in battle, rushed to Chinon in Anjou, where the Angevins kept vast quantities of money in their treasury. John seized the coffers and headed for England, where he had sufficient backing to take the English throne. He also managed to hold Normandy; but the king of France—saved from the jaws of death by the bolt that killed Richard - began to regain power and soon threatened Normandy. John fought bravely, but in a crucial battle in 1204 he lost the lands that Rollo the Viking had made his own three hundred years earlier.

Determined to win back all losses, John began taxing his English subjects heavily and amassing a vast war chest. By 1211 he had in his possession one half of all the coinage of England. His subjects, especially his barons, could take no more. They rebelled and, in 1215, forced John to sign Magna Carta and curtail the savage taxation. But John used some of his vast fortune to buy the services of foreign mercenary knights. They fought well for John, who soon had the Magna Carta rebels on the run.

As victory beckoned news came that the French king had landed in England with a large army. John campaigned successfully against invaders and rebels combined until two disasters struck - the loss of a very large war chest in The Wash ... and, at Stamford, Lincs, a bout of dysentery from which he did not recover.

JOHN'S SHORT CROSS COINAGE.

HENRICUS REX continued as the obverse legend throughout John's reign. However, on one-third of John's coins the letter **S** in the obverse legend is reversed as shown in the examples below. A single class from John's reign also depicts the king with a stubble beard. Fortunately it is one of those that has a reversed **S** so you will have no difficulty in distinguishing between the portraits of Richard and John.

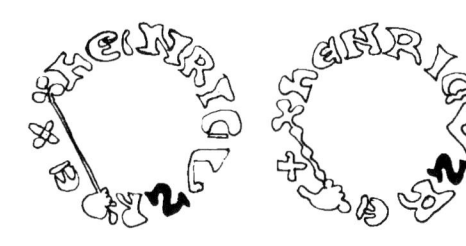

*A reversed **S** denotes ...*
a penny of king John.

HENRY III: 1216-1272

A boy of nine when his father died, Henry became monarch with Normandy already lost and half of England in the hands of a powerful French army. Could he survive?

His first asset lay in not being king John. His second lay in the appointment of William Marshall, earl of Pembroke, as regent. The earl's military skills turned the tide for the young monarch.

In fact the first act of the earl of Pembroke was to reissue Magna Carta and try for reconciliation between Henry and the barons who had opposed his father. But the barons fully expected the French to control all of England within weeks, so they declined to sign the charter. Pembroke responded with a crushing defeat of the French forces then besieging Lincoln. With the French now in retreat the earl issued another version of Magna Carta and this time succeeded in winning over the rebels.

England enjoyed a period a peace until Henry III became king in his own right aged twenty-five. Now his Angevin inheritance came to the fore with a bold plan to win back all the lost lands his family had once ruled. But Henry's schemes and the huge amounts of money he expended in bribes to foreign princes during the next thirty years of Continental intrigues cost him popularity at home. By 1264 rebel barons led by Simon de Montfort were besieging the king and his son Edward at Lewes. The barons won many concessions, kept Edward a virtual hostage for almost a year, and elected Simon de Montfort as Protector of England.

The Angevins - Henry III

But in 1265 prince Edward escaped, raised an army and defeated the rebels at the Battle of Evesham. De Montfort was captured, hanged, drawn and quartered. Henry III regained his throne and ruled in relative calm until his death in 1272.

HENRY III's SHORT CROSS COINAGE.

HENRICUS REX, once again a factually correct legend, remained unaltered until 1247. These coins differ little from those of the other Angevins; but on half of Henry III's short cross pennies the letter X in REX is altered quite distinctively from others in the series. The illustrations below show the three shapes in which the X appears on Henry III's short cross pennies:

A letter X like any of the three shown here indicates a penny of Henry III

A Final Discussion On Short Cross Issues

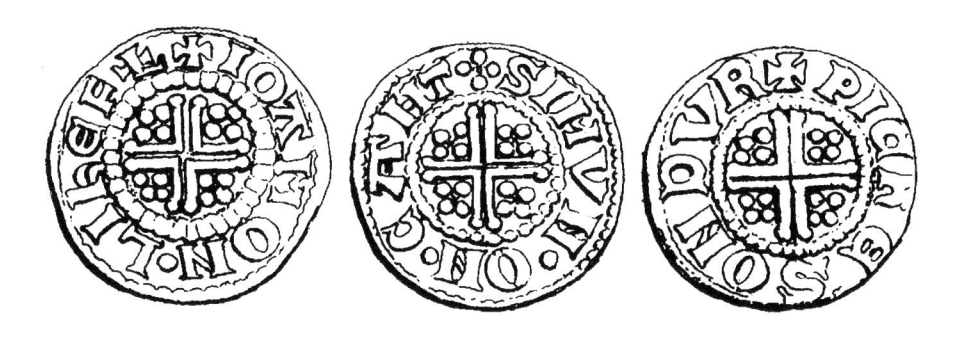

The Angevins - Henry III

A lot of Short Cross pennies are found worn and heavily clipped, like those found in an Angevin hoard in the 1980s and thought to have been deposited in the 1240s. The fact that such worn and heavily clipped specimens reached the hoard pot suggests this was a hoard of silver bullion valued by weight rather than a hoard of money to go back into circulation. It mattered little to a rich banker buying bullion that the silver consisted of barely recognizable coins; but for small traders and customers at the markets and fairs of Angevin England the state of the coinage became a matter of grave concern as Henry III's reign progressed.

By 1247, despite very infrequent newly minted issues, some short cross pennies had circulated for sixty-seven years and passed through innumerable hands. The temptation to take a hair's breadth in silver shavings from the edge of every coin as a safeguard against the next underweight penny foisted on them in a busy marketplace or rowdy tavern proved too much for many. Even innocent hands, roughened by harsh manual labour, took their toll on the king's portrait as money slipped through rasping fingers.

Pause a moment to reflect on an inexperienced collector's difficulties striving to identify pieces with half their letters clipped, and some of the remaining design rubbed to little more than a ghostly impression of what was struck at the mint. An advanced collector seeking a particular VF short cross penny from one of more than a dozen mints and as many as fifty moneyers (some of them at work during more than a single reign) has a reasonable chance of coping with such difficulties as blundered dies and obscure abbreviations because he/she will be looking at coins in the sort of condition shown in the row at the top of the previous page. But as a beginner you are far more likely to encounter short cross pennies looking more like those in the bottom row of the previous page. That's why it is advised that you content yourself at the outset, with the easier methods of identifying *some* of the short-cross pennies of the Angevins.

LONG CROSS COINAGE

With benefit of hindsight it's patently obvious that a short cross offered no protection from clippers with eyes on the peripheries of the coin. But with the arms of the voided cross extended to the very edges, and the two pellets at the ends of each arm retained, any person accepting a long cross penny could check with a glance that it had not suffered the attentions of cheats.

Other parts of the penny's design (discussed below) also changed on the new coinage; but a foolish decision to omit the moneyer's name and the mint town from the reverse so that the king's name and title could occupy obverse and reverse perimeters made the first issue highly unpopular. A coin without a moneyer as guarantor of its weight and fineness of silver harked back to the bad old days of the civil war. So the order went out for new dies to make long cross pennies bearing the name of the mint town on the reverse, but still leaving space for a shortened version of the king's legend to flow from the obverse. Predictably, the second type inspired as little confidence as the first. With several moneyers at work in busy mints it would have proved difficult to identify any culprit. At the third attempt both moneyer and mint town were restored to the reverse, while the king squeezed his abbreviated title onto the obverse.

The Angevins - Henry III

Public confidence in long cross pennies with moneyers' names and mint towns was restored and this reflects in the numerous hoards that have come to light. Many single long cross penny losses have also turned up thanks to metal detectorists. As a result, new collectors can now encounter examples for sale at affordable prices. The next page will help to increase your knowledge of the series by explaining a little more about the variety of legends found on them.

Advanced collectors distinguish up to seventeen classes within Henry III long cross pennies, differentiating them in some cases by minor variations in the shape of the king's face or crown. Beginners should have no difficulties in recognizing five classes by studying the legends and by determining whether or not the monarch holds a sceptre:

The Angevins - Henry III

HENRICUS REX is seen on the obverse of the Class 1A issue, which has the king's bust, with no sceptre. The reverse has the words **ANGLIE TERCI** (= THIRD OF ENGLAND) There is no moneyer's name or mint town. Only three pellets are seen in each quarter of ALL long cross pennies if this reign.

HENRICUS REX ANG is seen on the obverse of Class 1B, which also has no sceptre. The reverse has **LIE TERCI** as a continuation of the obverse legend, followed by either **LON ... CAN ...** or **... AED** for LONDON, CANTERBURY or BURY ST EDMUNDS.

HENRICUS REX TERCI is seen on the obverse of Class 2A. The reverse has the moneyer's name and mint.

HENRICUS REX III is seen on the obverse of Class 3A, with the reverse as previous.

HENRICUS REX III is also seen on Class 4A coins, but on these the king holds a sceptre.

The ten most common of more than twenty mint town are also worth recognizing in their abbreviated forms.

Look for the word ON, then use the list as a speedy reference to the ten mint towns you might encounter.
ON CANT shown at left.

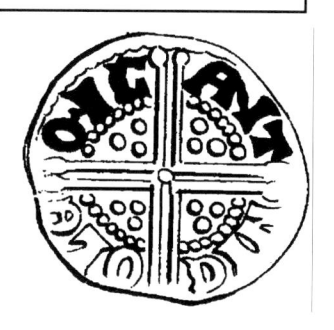

BRUSTOV = Bristol, a busy port and military stronghold throughout the reign. Four moneyers struck long cross pennies here.
SANTED = Bury St Edmunds, where five moneyers worked.
CANT = Canterbury, seat of the Archbishop. Up to ten moneyers worked here.
NICOLE = Lincoln, a military stronghold during the early years of the reign. Four moneyers.
LUND = London, increasing importance throughout the reign. At least ten moneyers.
NEVECA = Newcastle, major stronghold. Four moneyers.
NORHA = Northampton, major city with four moneyers.
NORWIC = Norwich, an important market. Four moneyers.
WINT = Winchester, the king's birthplace. Four moneyers.
EVERWIC = York, the leading northern city. Four moneyers.

Note: The long cross made halving and quartering to produce halfpence and farthings very popular; but in recent years a few round halfpence of Henry III have been uncovered.

The Plantagenets: 1272-1399

The name derives from the yellow sprig of wild broom - *planta genista* - used as a family crest by the earlier Angevins. But the four kings grouped by many historians as the Plantagenets (Edward I, Edward II, Edward III and Richard II) had in common a powerful determination to rule England, Wales, Ireland and Scotland as a united kingdom rather than expend most of their resources on attempts to win back lost Continental lands as the Angevins had done; though none altogether abandoned their claims to parts of what we now call France.

Tax revenues for wars, whether domestic or foreign, had now to be raised mainly on home territory. Thanks to Magna Carta, this called the monarch into negotiations with the fledgling Parliament. Kings had become accountable, and two of the four Plantagenets lost their crowns when called to account.

Edward I: 1272-1307

One of England's most successful soldier-kings. At twenty-two he fought and helped to defeat the rebel Simon de Montfort at the Battle of Evesham in 1265. Later he went as a crusader to the Holy Land where he won a major victory against Sultan Baybars; but Edward almost died when a Muslim assassin struck him with a poisoned dagger. Only the swift actions of Edward's beautiful wife, Eleanor of Castile, who sucked the poison from the wound, saved the prince's life.

When Henry III died in 1272 Edward, now king but still in the Holy Land, made a slow journey back to England via his dukedom in Aquitaine where he secured his borders against the French. Once home he embarked on one of his most successful exploits: the conquest of Wales. He soon destroyed the Welsh princes and gave the title Prince of Wales to his own son, then set about building a ring of strong castles around the Welsh coasts.

The Plantagenets - Edward I

In 1296 he marched his army into Scotland where the nobles were squabbling over the crown. Edward fought his way to Elgin, took possession of the sacred Stone of Scone, declared the country an English dependency, and earned himself the nickname *Hammer of The Scots*.

The long-cross pennies that his father, Henry III, had introduced continued into this reign generally unaltered in style. But one obvious difference should help the inexperienced collector recognize Edward's coins, namely the hair style has a more naturalistic appearance with wavy locks rather than the tight curls seen on the coins of his father's reign. This applies even to the earliest coins of Edward which must have circulated before the king arrived in England after his foreign travels. In fact these pieces were struck with the name *Henricus*, even though their crude portraits are certainly of Edward I.

HIII   EDI

Examples of Continental Black Money circulating illegally in England during the 13th century

The very poor quality of those first coins gives a quite misleading impression of the new king's attitude towards monetary matters and England's economy. In fact he possessed business and fiscal skills to match his military prowess.

On his journey home he negotiated a massive contract to supply English wool to the weavers of the Low Countries. He also witnessed the contempt and mistrust that so many debased and underweight Continental coins faced. He vowed that English coins would not suffer

The Plantagenets - Edward I

the same fate, determined that low-grade Continental *black money* (= very low-grade silver) or *esterlings* would not circulate in his dominions.

It took four years of frantic work by Edward's engravers and mint masters before the king could fulfil those vows. Then - in 1279 - he decreed that every subject must carry their money to the nearest mint and exchange it for the newly-made coins which now became the nation's legal tender. The new denominations, shown actual size, were:

The Groat (26-29mm)

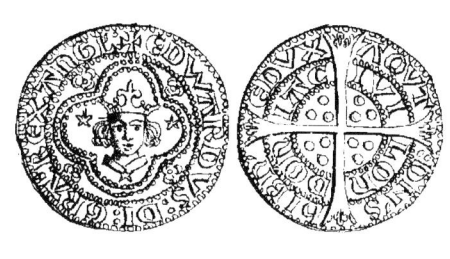

The Traditional Penny (19-22mm)

The Halfpenny (14-16mm)

The Farthing (10-12mm)

Groats derived their name from the Latin *grossus* meaning *thick* and the Continental coin, the *gros tournois,* a coin of similar size. Groats were the largest silver coins to circulate in England up to 1279;

Legend reads:
EDWARDUS
DI GRA REX
ANGL = Edward
By The Grace of God,
King of England

Outer Reverse
Legend reads:
DNS HIBNE
DUX AQUT
= Lord Of
Ireland Duke Of
Aquitaine

Inner Reverse
Legend reads:
CIVI LONDONIA =
City Of London

Although admired for their appearance, the groat proved unpopular with foreign merchants who preferred to receive four pennies rather than a four-penny groat which in fact contained a little less silver. Poorer folk had no time for groats owing to the problems they caused with change. But this new English coin became very popular as jewellery. Large numbers were gilded and mounted as brooches. However, that was not what the king had in mind, so very few groats were minted during his reign - hence their high cost today. Some have been found by metal detectorists; but beginner-collectors are unlikely to spend over one thousand pounds asked for even F-grade specimens. Nevertheless, the illustration of the groat on the previous page should be studied because the newly introduced smaller coins had several similarities.

The new pennies with their realistic full-face regal portrait on the obverse, and their bold long cross on the reverse (a continuing strong deterrent against clipping) delighted all who handled them, in England and abroad. Indeed the appearance of English silver pennies was scarcely to alter during the next two hundred years. Add the high quality of their silver content and weight and it's easy to appreciate why so many of Edward I's new pennies went to the Continent and did not return.

Almost all the dozen or so penny types depict a crown with three prongs at each end. (See a few examples on the next page. Experts refer to it as a *tri-foliate crown*. The next monarch, Edward II, nearly always wears a bi-foliate two-pronged crown.)

The Plantagenets - Edward I

Almost all Edward I pennies have an obverse legend that begins with
EDWR
whereas the pennies of Edward II usually have
EDWA.
The full obverse legends will be something close to
EDW REX ANGL DNS HYB
= Edward King Of England Lord Of Ireland.

The following (reverse legend) mint names appear on **Edward I** pennies but not on **Edward II** pennies:

VILL BRISTOLIE (Bristol); **CIVITAS CESTRIE** (Chester); **CIVITAS EXONIE** (Exeter); **VIL KYNCESTON** (Hull); **CIVITAS LINCOL** (Lincoln); **VIL NOV CASTRI** (Newcastle);
CIVITAS EBORACI (York)
Other mints - at Canterbury, Durham, Bury-St-Edmunds, London and Berwick - were used by Edward I and II. They are usually written as **CANTOR, DVNELM, SCI EDMUNDI, LONDON, BERREWYCI.**

Although Edward I was not the first monarch to introduce halfpence and farthings, he was the first to do so with some success. Previously there appears to have been a near-total monetary disregard for the needs of the poor, whose daily lives revolved around earning and exchanging the lowest denomination coins. As we have seen, in earlier reigns a poor man or woman in need of a farthing in change after buying a loaf costing three-farthings had no option but to accept a one-quarter segment of a whole penny cut for the purpose. In recent years large numbers of these easily lost cut quarters and halves dating earlier than 1279 have been found, with a few unexpected rare whole halfpence and farthings of earlier reigns also turning up.

ENGLANDS' STRIKING HISTORY

The Plantagenets - Edward I

Cutting pennies into segments occurred even in Edward I's reign despite the generous minting of his whole halfpence and farthings.

These deliberately cut pieces are easy to recognize: the cuts will always follow the line of the long-cross on the penny's reverse, whereas a coin sliced accidentally by a plough's blade is cut at random.

If you learn to recognize the legends shown clearly on the previous page you should be able to spot an Edward I cut-half or cut-quarter penny, provided the piece has not suffered greatly from the attentions of clippers. Quarter segments cut from pennies have three pellets.

If you encounter a tiny but unclipped cut-quarter piece that has just one pellet in its segment you might have a fragment originally cut from a halfpenny that was struck at the Newcastle mint. Full halfpennies and full farthings from Newcastle all had only four pellets in total on their reverse sides. The reverse legend reads "**NOVI CASTRI**" - Latin for Newcastle.

The obverse portrait of Edward I on his Newcastle farthings depicts a face that is somewhat longer than on other coins of the reign. The legend on his Newcastle halfpence and farthings reads:

EDW R ANGL DNS HYB
= EDWARD KING OF ENGLAND LORD OF IRELAND.

Obverse legends on farthings read either **EDWARDUS REX** or
E R ANGLI - EDWARD KING OF ENGLAND.

Some mints omitted the inner beaded circle on the obverse of their farthings

Unbeaded

Beaded

Edward II: 1307-1327

A lonely child whose mother died when he was six, Edward's first adolescent friendship was with a Gascoigne nobleman's son named Piers Gaveston. On hearing rumours of homosexuality, Edward I had Gaveston banished; but when the old king died one year later Edward II recalled Gaveston and invested him as Duke of Cornwall.

The Plantagenets - Edward II

Aged twenty-three at the time, Edward reluctantly fulfilled his dynastic responsibilities by marrying Isabella of France and siring a son, but he preferred Gaveston's company and dallied in Cornwall while Robert the Bruce invaded northern England. An inevitable revolt by his barons forced the king to send his friend to France. And when Gaveston slipped back into England a few years later he was captured by angry barons and beheaded.

In 1314 Edward finally led an army deep into Scotland, only to see it cut to ribbons at Bannockburn. The king returned to England and to another homosexual affair with his royal chamberlain. When the Earl of Lancaster led a revolt Edward achieved one of his few military successes, defeating Lancaster's army at Boroughbridge in 1322 and later putting dozens of rebel barons to death.

In 1325 Isabella visited France with her adolescent son (the future Edward III) and was soon embroiled in a plot to overthrow her husband. She landed with a small army a year later and quickly gathered massive support. Edward II and his chamberlain fled London but were captured a few days later. With his supporters all dead, the king abdicated in favour of his son. A rumour has long persisted that Edward II eventually died while in captivity in a ritualistic killing in which a red hot poker was thrust into his backside!

The Plantagenets - Edward II

Edward II's coinage differs little from his father's, though no groats were minted in this reign, while the pennies and scarcer whole halfpence and farthings are all slightly smaller, though relative size is difficult to judge because some clipping still went on despite the long crosses. Train your eye to spot Edward II's distinctive bifoliate crowns which appear on almost all of his coins. Bear in mind that it is at each end of the crown where the two prongs appear. The central area of the crown is of less importance when making the distinction.

CROWN	REVERSE LEGEND					
	V	C	V	C	C	C
	I	I	I	I	I	I
	L	V	L	V	V	V
	S	I	L	I	I	I
	C	T	A	T	T	T
	I	A	B	A	A	A
	E	S	E	S	S	S
	D	D	R	C	D	L
	M	V	R	A	V	O
	V	N	E	N	R	N
	N	E	W	T	E	D
	D	L	Y	O	M	O
	I	M	C	R	E	N
	Bury St Edmunds	Durham (1)	Berwick on Tweed	Canterbury	Durham (2)	London
	MUST BE EDWARD II		PROBABLY EDWARD II IF BIFOLIATE CROWN			

Omission of the moneyer's name from the reverse side of coinage when Edward I introduced his new currency in 1275 seems to imply that all moneyers working at a particular mint would henceforth be held responsible for errors or underweight coins.

However, it was at this time that the mintmarks and privy marks discussed at the beginning of the book came to prominence. Instead of stamping his name on his work, each moneyer was assigned a tiny emblem, or a shape of crown, or a hairstyle, or some other difference that identified his dies just as clearly as if he had signed his name in full.

Advanced collectors use these minor variations far more than newcomers to coin collecting - not simply because they have greater knowledge, but also because they are usually handling coins in better than F-grade. On coins of F-grade or lower the moneyer's marks have often worn away. A lot of the wear occurred back in the 13th century, but it was during its first few months of circulation, when the privy marks would have been quite prominent to officials in the know, that any cheating by a moneyer would have come to light.

Beginners can identify many of Edward II's coins with a fair degree of certainty by using the diagram on the previous page. A coin with a bifoliate crown and the abbreviation for the Bury St Edmunds mint, or for the Durham mint with spelling (1) *must* be an Edward II coin. The other four mints produced coins of Edward I and II with the same reverse lettering; but only Edward II will have the bifoliate crown.

EDWARD III: 1327-1377

He was brought to England from France at fourteen by his mother for the sole purpose of fomenting revolt against his father, Edward II. Then the old queen used him as a puppet figurehead while she and her lover drained the royal coffers and signed peace treaties with Scotland and France to England's great disadvantage. It was not an auspicious beginning for the king who would rule England for fifty years.

The Plantagenets - Edward III

On his eighteenth birthday Edward - now with a young queen and a newly born son - showed himself a man of action. Supported by a group of close friends, he ambushed and imprisoned his mother's lover, then formally announced that he had assumed full royal powers. He also revealed plans to invade Scotland and replace the Scottish king with a man of his choosing - Edward Balliol.

Northern barons, disgruntled at the loss of lands in Lowland Scotland as a result of the old queen's peace treaty, flocked to Edward III's banner. The two armies met at Halidon Hill near Berwick-on-Tweed where the English routed the Scottish army. In a second battle near Durham a few years later Edward captured the Scottish king.

With northern Britain secured, the young king turned his attention to France where the English won spectacular victories at Crécy and Calais. Only the outbreak of the Black Death prevented Edward from seizing all of France. And when the English returned eight years later as the plague subsided, another defeat was inflicted on the French at Poitiers, where the French king was captured.

ENGLANDS' STRIKING HISTORY

The Plantagenets - Edward III

With two kings as his prisoners, Edward, by then approaching fifty and perhaps tired of warfare, turned to diplomacy. He eventually agreed to massive ransoms for the two monarchs on condition that his ancestral lands in Aquitaine were secured, and that Calais was declared an English port. But the final decade of his life brought disappointments. The death of his eldest son cast doubts about the succession, with the named heir - his grandson Richard - likely to face a challenge from the king's third son, John of Gaunt.

Edward III had no control over monetary affairs during the early part of his reign when pennies and halfpennies almost identical to those of Edward II were issued. But the increasing volume of trade between England and her allies in the Low Countries later in the reign required the introduction of high value gold coins and an accompanying range of silver denominations of which the most successful was the groat:

This newly designed coin differed from the unsuccessful groat of Edward I in having the king's bust within a frame of nine segments, compared with the Edward I type, shown above right.

The Plantagenets - Edward III

Legends on Edward III coinage record his ceaseless struggles to rule a united Britain and to hold lands across the Channel. The new groat had on the obverse:

EDWARD D G REX ANGL Z FRANC D HYB
(EDWARD BY THE GRACE OF GOD KING OF ENGLAND AND FRANCE AND LORD OF IRELAND)

The reverse was largely taken up by:

POSVI DEUM ADIVTOREM MEUM
CIVITAS LONDON
(I HAVE MADE GOD MY HELPER)
(CITY OF LONDON)

New groats were also struck at York, their reverse legend having: **CIVITAS EBORACI**

The obverse altered later to:

EDWAR DEI GRAC REX ANGL
(EDWARD BY THE GRACE OF GOD KING OF ENGLAND)

... only to change again to:

EDWARD DEI GRA REX ANGL FRANC
(EDWARD BY THE GRACE OF GOD KING OF ENGLAND FRANCE)

.... then to: **EDWARD DI G REX ANGL F DNS HIB A**
(EDWARD BY THE GRACE OF GOD KING OF ENGLAND FRANCE LORD OF IRELAND AQUITAINE)

Even more interesting were the English coins struck in Calais when Edward took possession. They have a slightly different obverse legend and a reverse bearing the name:

VILLA CALESIE (TOWN OF CALAIS)

The Plantagenets - Edward III

The acceptance of his new half-groat, or two-penny piece, reflects rising agricultural incomes following the Black Death when a quarter or the entire population died and labour shortage forced many landlords to offer money wages to peasants for the first time. At a size slightly larger than the modern British penny when unclipped, the half-groat remained a popular coin for more than three hundred years. Two other kings named Edward were to issue them, but most Edward III half-groats have the name EDWARDUS in full within their obverse legends, whereas later monarchs used EDWARD.

Half-groats and the larger groats are almost identical in design; but Edward III's pennies differ markedly, not only from those denominations, but also from earlier pennies in one very important respect: the hairstyle, which is described variously as *bushy, flowing, unkempt*. For beginners likely to encounter clipped pennies it is useful as an identification guide. Any hammered silver penny with a front-facing portrait of a king of youthful appearance and with hair reminiscent of a 60's pop star should be considered a penny of Edward III in the absence of other evidence to the contrary.

The Plantagenets - Edward III

Edward III was the first monarch in English history to issue generous supplies of both halfpennies and farthings in attempts to meet the needs of his poorer subjects. Yet despite the millions that must have been minted, they are scarce today and there never seemed enough to go round back in the 14th century. A glance at this illustration shows why:

Farthing, halfpenny and penny obverse of Edward III shown at their actual size when minted.

The long crosses on the two small coins confirm that no clipping took place while they circulated, probably because they went quickly into hoards. The two ENLARGED illustrations of a typical well-circulated farthing and halfpenny from this reign are shown here, BOTH at double actual size:

Clipped farthing actual size   *...and 3x size.*

Clipped halfpenny actual size   *...... and 3x size*

ENGLANDS' STRIKING HISTORY

The Plantagenets - Edward III

We now know, thanks to coins unearthed, that numerous losses occurred when work-callused fingers handled worn and clipped farthings and halfpennies. Even more surprising is that coin cutting still went on, especially the cutting of halfpennies to make farthings. Fortunately that unkempt hairstyle of the king can help you to recognize even a clipped coin from this reign.

Many obverses have **CIVITAS LONDON,** while some of the lettering of **EDWARDUS REX** (KING EDWARD) or less commonly **EDWARDUS REX A** (EDWARD KING OF ENGLAND) in combination with hairstyle and the size of the coin can also help when it comes to identification of poorer than F-grade specimens.

Despite their small size and occasionally blundered legends these Edward III halfpennies and farthings won trust in the marketplaces of England and the Continent thanks to the fineness of the silver from which most were struck. But the temptation to mint and circulate inferior copies drew in millions of lower grade pieces from overseas. As a defence against the charge of forgery these Continental copies usual had a legend reading **EDWARDIENSIS.**

You may hear experienced numismatists speaking of *Gresham's Law* in this context. They refer to medieval economist, Sir Thomas Gresham, who told Queen Elizabeth I that "good and bad coin cannot circulate together because inferior money remains in circulation, while coins made from fine gold or silver tend to go into hoards, or to end up in foreign lands." That's what happened to many of Edward III's halfpennies and farthings.

RICHARD II: 1377-1399

Just as we associate King John with Magna Carta, we *ought* to associate Richard II with the Peasants Revolt of 1381; but it's the peasant leader's name, Watt Tyler, that we recall, not the king's.

The son of the Black Prince and Joan Plantagenet, the Fair Maid of Kent, he became king at ten, and at fourteen met Watt Tyler at Smithfield to discuss rebel demands. His companion, the mayor of London, took matters into his own hands and fatally stabbed Watt Tyler as the young king looked on. The rebel mob dispersed and Richard II took the credit for defending his kingdom.

The praise seems to have gone to his head because he spent the remainder of his reign insisting on his divine right to impose taxes and to live in a make-believe world of chivalry and courtly extravagance. He had a bodyguard of highly skilled archers who accompanied him even to sittings of Parliament, especially when Richard went there to demand higher taxes.

Inevitably he made enemies, especially his uncle, John of Gaunt, who as third son of Edward III had some claim to the throne. When his uncle died, Richard felt sufficiently secure on his throne to take himself and his bodyguard to Ireland. In his absence Gaunt's son - Henry Bolingbroke - landed in England and claimed the throne. Richard II rushed homeward, but was captured and forced to abdicate. He died a prisoner in Pontefract castle.

The Plantagenets - Richard II

Groat, halfgroat, penny, halfpenny and farthing issues continued little altered in this reign, but the monarch's name change, after three Edwards, makes spotting a Richard II coin fairly easy provided clipping has not removed too much of the obverse legend. On groats it reads:

RICARD DI GRA REX ANGL Z FR
or
RICARD DI GRA REX ANGLIE Z FRANC
(RICHARD BY THE GRACE OF GOD KING OF ENGLAND AND FRANCE)

The reverse has:
POSVI DEUM ADIVTORE MEU
or
POSVI DEUM ADIVTOREM MEUM
(I HAVE MADE GOD MY HELPER)

On halfgroats the obverse legend is shortened to:
RICARD DI GRA REX ANGL

Only the London mint produced groats and halfgroats, so on both coins the inner circle of lettering on the reverse reads:

CIVITAS LONDON

You will encounter greater variety on penny reverses because that denomination alone came from London, York and Durham, with York by far the most prolific mint. Look for:

CIVITAS LONDON or **CIVITAS EBORACI** or **CIVITAS DUNOLM**

A further aid to identification of the York issues is a quatrefoil device in the centre of the long cross, as shown in the illustration above right. Most pennies have obverse legends commencing:

RICARDUS REX ANG

Halfpennies and farthings were minted only in London, so on reverses look for:

CIVITAS LONDON

These two denominations often turn up in clipped and worn condition. Nevertheless you might spot the rare issue shown above right (enlarged) which has roses instead of the usual three pellets in the quarters of its long cross.

A Few Words On Sterlings, Esterlings And Medieval Bullion Smuggling

As a metal for minting coins, pure silver has a grave disadvantage: softness that causes rapid wear of any coin in general circulation. To overcome that drawback mints have always added, or alloyed, a small quantity of other metal to increase silver's durability. It follows that the weight of a silver coin does not tell its true value. The percentage of the base metal added to it must also be known. We can then state the percentage of silver as the coin's purity, otherwise known as its FINENESS.

Offa, king of Mercia, issued the first silver coins minted in England, in the year 760. He decreed that one pound of silver should be minted into 240 pennies. But thanks to a gradual reduction of fineness the value of a penny dwindled inexorably during subsequent centuries.

The first king to order a devaluation was William I. In 1067 he established a new mint at the Tower of London and decreed that it would make its 240 pennies from a Tower pound of silver rather than from a Troyes pound which was 6.5% heavier. William I also ordered the reduction of Tower silver's purity to 925 parts per thousand. This became known as STERLING SILVER, and coins were made from silver of this standard right up to the 20th century. During the early medieval centuries English pennies were known throughout Europe as sterlings.

Unlike English monarchs, continental kings and princes allowed barons, even cities, to mint their own coinage. Many copied the designs seen on English sterlings to ensure acceptance of their money. Some, knowing the perennial shortage of halfpennies and farthings in England, produced copies of sterlings containing a half or a quarter of the silver. These copies, soon referred to as esterlings, and sometimes called by their local names (crockards, pollards, eagles, lionines, staldings, etc.) or, thanks to their dark colour due to low silver content, as black money, found their way to England in huge numbers, where they circulated in local markets as substitutes for halfpennies and farthings. In some instances when their silver content was fairly high, they could be passed on to the unwary as genuine English money.

The practice grew up of foreign merchants bringing Continental goods to England and insisting on unclipped sterlings in payment; then shipping the sterlings across the Channel and melting them down to produce esterlings. This went on during most reigns we have so far discussed. Kings raged against what they saw as bullion smugglers. They passed laws, appointed searchers to check outgoing baggage at ports, made examples of the few they caught. But money smuggling continued.

One monarch who achieved a resounding, if temporary, victory was Edward III. In 1335 he issued, with no advance warning, a substantial coinage of halfpennies and farthings at .833 fineness - lower than the equivalent esterlings. The smugglers were unable to offload their foreign money. But English halfpenny and farthing minting soon dried up. The smugglers were back in business until wars and plagues killed off much foreign trade.

THE LANCASTRIANS: 1399-1461

Because Henry Bolingbroke was legal heir to the duchy of Lancaster before he became king, the name House of Lancaster is applied to a dynasty that included Henry IV, V and VI - father, son and grandson - who occupied England's throne for the next sixty-odd years. These were often years of rebellion and instability, interspersed by short-lived victories against France and rival claimants to the throne. This was the dynasty that gave England success at Agincourt, yet later pitched the nation into the Wars of the Roses to test whether the succession should keep to the male line or could pass through females. This was also the dynasty that burned Joan of Arc and finally lost all but Calais as its Continental possessions.

HENRY IV: 1399-1413

He spent the early part of his reign defending his crown. In 1403 the Percys of Northumberland, turned against him and conspired with Owen Glendower. But Henry defeated them at the Battle of Shrewsbury and later executed many of the rebels. By 1408 he had gained firm control of the country.

Throughout Henry IV's reign currency smuggling continued until a serious shortage of bullion in 1412 obliged the king to order a reduction in the weight of his coins - by 16% in the case of silver. So we have heavy and light coinages in this reign, though no groats were struck until the light period of 1412-1413.

A light groat of 1412. Note the cross pattée in the obverse legend right at the top. Most Henry IV coins have this mintmark.

GROAT

The obverse legend reads:
HENRIC DI GRA REX ANGLE ..or.. HENRIC DI GRA REX ANGLE Z FRAC[IE]
and on the reverse:
POSVI DEUM ADIVTOREM MEUM CIVITAS LONDON
because only the London mint produced groats.

HALFGROAT

Halfgroats were issued during both heavy and light periods - all by the London mint. They differ little from groats, other than in size, but there are minor differences in the obverse legends on the heavy and light issues:
HENRIC DI GRA REX ANGL Z FRANC
suggests a heavy halfgroat of 1399-1412.

HENRIC DI GRA REX ANG Z
suggests a light halfgroat of 1412-1413.

The penny, halfpenny and farthing issues of this reign can cause confusion for beginners faced with worn and clipped specimens yet eager to identify them from the range of tiny marks usually discussed at length in more advanced numismatic works. Here we shall limit the information to main obverse legends, mint names and major variations that the ravages of time may not have worn completely from the coin's surface. Absolute beginners will probably be happy to confirm that they have a Lancastrian monarch's coin in their hands.

PENNY.

Most of the HEAVY pennies will have the obverse legend:
HENRIC DI GRA REX ANGL
Most reverses have: **CIVITAS LONDON**
and a long cross with **FOUR** pellets in two of the quarters, and **THREE** pellets in the other two. Note however that some heavy pennies have only three pellets in all four quarters of the reverse.

There are YORK mint heavy pennies with the obverse as above, but with:
CIVITAS EBORACI
and a quatrefoil at the centre of the reverse cross.

Most LIGHT pennies (1412-1413) have the obverse legend:
HENRIC REX ANGLI
with a pellet or an annulet on each side of the king's crown.
Most LONDON reverses have: **CIVITAS LONDON**
with only **THREE** pellets in each quarter.
YORK's light pennies have the same obverse as LONDON, with an annulet after **HENRIC.** The reverse is the same as the YORK heavy pennies, again with a quatrefoil at the centre of the cross.
DURHAM also issued light pennies with an obverse legend as for LONDON and a trefoil on the king's breast. The reverse reads:
CIVITAS DVNOLM

HALFPENNY & FARTHING.

Heavy or light, almost all have **HENRIC REX ANGL** on the obverse, and **CIVITAS LONDON** on the reverse, with THREE pellets in each quarter.

HENRY V: 1413 - 1422

At sixteen he commanded knights and archers at the Battle of Shrewsbury (1403) and later took charge of the entire Welsh campaign, forcing Owen Glendower's submission a few years later. When he became king at twenty-six his reputation as a soldier already echoed throughout Europe. Soon he began stockpiling ships and supplies on the south coast, while the French hurriedly prepared for all-out war.

But as William Shakespeare showed us so vividly in his drama, the new king had old enemies in his own ranks. He narrowly escaped assassination by the earls of March and Cambridge, secret supporters of the Plantagenet cause. Henry V showed no mercy; all the rebels were at once rounded up and hanged. Then the young king crossed the Channel on a campaign that took his English archers to Agincourt where they annihilated the flower of French aristocracy. Several years of warfare, diplomacy and a marriage to the French king's daughter eventually brought Henry V to within reach of his cherished goal. He would have become king of England *and* France when the French king died in October, 1422. Alas, an outbreak of dysentery claimed Henry V's life two months earlier.

The need for sound finances and sufficient tax revenues to sustain his armies persuaded Henry V to continue with the light coinage introduced by his father. The coins altered very little, though a strict system of mintmarks and other privy marks ensured that standards remained high. Advanced collectors use the marks to accurately date Henry V coins. For our purposes the following pointers will prove useful and help you to identify most of this monarch's groats, halfgroats, pennies, halfpennies and farthings.

As a general observations, the words most commonly used to describe portraits of Henry V on his coinage are *emaciated, scowling, frowning and narrow-necked*. Keep those words in mind when you examine any hammered silver piece you suspect might date from the 15th century. Even on worn coins a grim-looking face and a scrawny neck will catch your eye.

The Lancastrians - Henry V

A Scrawny Neck

Annulets

Cross with Pellet

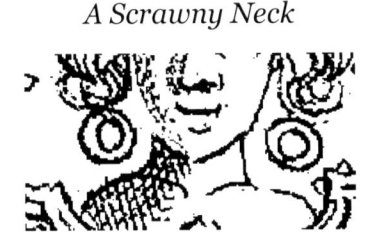

Flighty Hair

Many portraits show the king with wisps of hair protruding from beneath his crown. Other kings in this dynasty had good heads of hair; but on Henry V's issues the stray hairs are very noticeable, though not so much on worn coins.

We have already seen that Henry IV often has a cross patée in the obverse legend at a position just above his crown. On Henry V coinage this is often (though not always) altered to show the cross with a pellet or annulet at its centre.

In this reign mint marks and privy marks including mullets (5-pointed stars) and annulets became increasingly important. They sometimes occur within legends, but when they appear in the field of the coin, either alongside the crown, or at the sides of the face, they stand out clearly.

Any one of the aforementioned features can occur in other reigns; but if three or four occur together on a coin, suspect that it might be a Henry V issue.

GROAT

Most obverse legends read:
HENRIC DI GRA REX ANGL Z FRANC
The reverse reads:
POSVI DEUM ADIVITOREM MEUM CIVITAS LONDON
On some groats a mullet (5-pointed star) is shown on the king's breast. On others a trefoil appears in the obverse legend after POSVI.

HALFGROAT

The obverse reads: **HENRIC DI GRA REX ANGL Z F**

The reverse reads: **POSVI DEUM ADIVTOREM MEU[M] CIVITAS LONDON**

The scrawny necks referred to earlier seem especially pronounced on halfgroats.

PENNY
The obverse reads: **HENRIC REX ANGL**
or: **HENRIC DI GRA REX ANGL**

Annulets, or pellets, or mullets or trefoils can usually be seen somewhere in the field.

This penny has an annulet and a mullet close to the crown.

Three mints issued Henry V pennies: London, York and Durham. Reverses have one of the following:
CIVITAS LONDON
CIVITAS EBORACI (York)
CIVITAS DUNOLM (Durham)

The York penny has a quatrefoil in the centre of the reverse long cross.

HALFPENNY & FARTHING

These have identical obverse and reverse lettering to the LONDON

HENRY VI 1422-1461 & 1470-1471

Born at Windsor Castle, Henry VI succeeded to the crowns of England and France before the age of one, when his father Henry V and his grandfather Charles VI of France died within months of each other. But the dual monarchy proved too difficult to maintain. Victories by Joan of Arc began to weaken England's grip on France. Normandy was lost in 1450.

Those failures led to civil war in England between Yorkist and Lancastrian factions. Pitted against Henry was the Duke of York, asserting his legitimate claim to the throne descended as he was, through his mother, from Edward III. The Wars of the Roses were thus a struggle to decide if the succession could pass through females. But the Duke of York was killed at the Battle of Wakefield in 1460.

However, in 1461, his eighteen-year-old son Edward, an able commander, defeated the Lancastrians at the Battle of Towton (Of 120,000 men who fought, 28,000 died).

The Lancastrians - Henry VI

London opened it's gates to the Yorkist forces. Henry fled to Scotland, but was captured and imprisoned in the Tower of London in 1465. Briefly restored to the throne in 1470, he lost the Battle of Tewkesbury in 1471. Edward of York became Edward VI and Henry VI was put to death in the Tower of London.

Because examples of groats, halfgroats, pennies and halfpennies from this reign can be bought relatively cheaply, Henry VI coinage offers new collectors opportunities to venture beyond obverse and reverse legends and confidently expect to find clues that will date most pieces to within a few years. That's because the king and his mint-masters developed privy marks to a sophisticated level; combining them with mintmarks and with variations in lettering as well as portraits.

The illustration at right shows the ten marks most likely to survive even on coins of lower than f-grade. Top row left to right are: ANNULET, LIS, TREFOIL, ROSETTE, MASCLE. Bottom row left to right are: PINECONE, LEAF, PELLET, VOIDED CROSS, RESTORATION CROSS.

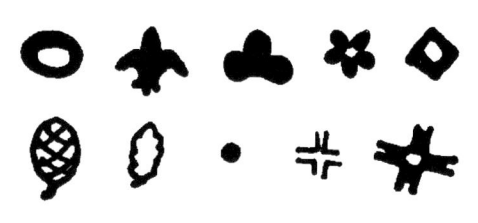

They can be found, singly or in combinations, within the legends, or close to the monarch's portrait within the field. Look closely at the two groats depicted above to see how many you can spot. Use a magnifying glass, an essential part of any collector's kit, which will give excellent results when used on our illustrations. After viewing the marks depicted on these pages you will sharpen your eyes for spotting identical marks on F-grade, even worn pieces, encountered in dealers' trays.

GROAT

Almost all groats have the obverse legend:
HENRIC DI GRA REX ANGL Z FRANC
and the reverse:
POSVI DEUM ADIVTOREM MEUM
with **CIVITAS LONDON or VILLA CALISIE or CIVITAS EBORACI** depending on the mint town.

If you can see **ONE ANNULET IN TWO OF THE QUARTERS** as shown at right, the groat dates from 1422 - 1427.

If you can see a **LIS TO LEFT AND RIGHT OF THE KING'S NECK** (as shown at right) the coin was minted in York. **ANNULETS AT THE SIDE OF THE NECK** indicate the Calais mint.

If you can see **ROSETTES AND MASCLES** within the legends on both sides, the groat dates from 1427-1430. (Issued by London and by Calais.)

If you can see **PINECONES AND MASCLES** within the legends on both sides, the groat dates from 1430-1434. (Issued by London and by Calais.)

If you can see **A MASCLE AND A LEAF** within the legends on both sides, the groat dates from 1434-1435. (Issued by London and by Calais.)

If you can see a **LEAF ON THE KING'S BREAST, AND TREFOILS** within the legend, the groat dates from 1435-1438. (Issued by London and by Calais.)

The Lancastrians - Henry VI

If you can see a **LEAF ON THE KING'S BREAST, AND TREFOILS** on each side of the king's neck, and a **TREFOIL OF PELLETS** within the obverse legend, *as in the example below left,* the groat dates from 1438-1443. (Issued by London and by Calais.)

And if you can see **A LEAF ON THE KING'S BREAST, A PELLET AT BOTH SIDES OF THE CROWN, AND AN EXTRA PELLET IN TWO OF THE FOUR REVERSE QUARTERS,** as above left, the groat dates from 1445-1454.

HALFGROAT

All halfgroats have the obverse legend:
HENRIC DI GRA REX ANGL Z FR
and the reverse:
POSVI DEUM ADIVTOREM MEU[M]
with **CIVITAS LONDON or VILLA CALISIE or CIVITAS EBORACI** depending on the mint town.

Annulets, pellets, trefoils, rosettes, mascles, pinecones and leaves were all used as privy marks in similar ways to their use on groats.

PENNY, HALFPENNY, FARTHING

These smaller denominations have as their obverse legend:
HENRICUS REX ANGLIE

And, like the groats and halfgroats, they have privy marks including annulets, rosettes, mascles, pinecones and leaves which can date a coin very accurately.

The Lancastrians - Henry VI

If you encounter a penny, halfpenny or farthing with the legend:
HENRIC DI GRA REX ANGL - it's a piece dating from the period of Henry VI's second reign, 1470-1471.

THE YORKISTS: 1461-1485

The House of York's claimants to the throne of England were all descended from Richard, Duke of York, whose symbol was a white rose. Their conquest of the red rose Lancastrians in 1461 did not put an end to the Wars of the Roses, which rumbled on until the start of the sixteenth century. Family disloyalties played a large part in York's downfall, though reconciliation was finally achieved between the warring houses as a result of a marriage which combined white and red rose emblems to establish an entirely new dynasty.

EDWARD IV 1461-1470 & 1471-1483

As the first Yorkist to occupy England's throne, the new king, aged just eighteen, made a bold decision to march north from London in the winter of 1461 and attempt to engage Henry of Lancaster in combat and kill him. The two armies met at Towton, Yorkshire, scene of the bloodiest battle ever to take place on British soil because in the parley beforehand both sides agreed that no quarter would be given or asked, as each hoped to end the Wars of the Roses there and then. Edward fought in the front rank to encourage his soldiers, a gamble that paid with victory, though the Lancastrian king escaped to Scotland.

Edward IV showed himself equally bold in monetary affairs. At a time when bullion smuggling rose to unprecedented heights as the value of Continental currencies fell, he reduced the weight of English sterlings by twenty percent and minted huge quantities of new coins. He built close relationships with London's merchants and made a fortune from dealing in wool.

The Yorkists - Edward IV

His coins included:

GROAT

Both heavy and light issues have on their obverse:
EDWARD DI GRA REX ANGL Z FRANC

The reverse reads: **POSVI DEUM ADIVTOREM MEUM**

All heavy groats (1461-1465) have: **CIVITAS LONDON**
because only the London mint operated during those years, but there were several heavy issues with different privy and other marks including lis, pellet, crescent, quatrefoil, trefoil and annulet.

Heavy groat with crescent on breast and quatrefoils to left and right of neck. Reverse has CIVITAS LONDON.

Light groats (1464-1470) were struck at London, Bristol, Coventry, Norwich and York, so reverse legend might have:
CIVITAS LONDON, VILLA BRESTOLL (or BRISTOLL), CIVITAS COVETRE, CIVITAS NORWIC (or NORVIC) or CIVITAS EBORACI
Again a variety of privy marks were used on the light groats. Additionally the letters: **B, C, N and E**
occur on the king's breast on coins minted in Bristol, Coventry, Norwich and York.

A Norwich light groat, with 'n' on breast and CIVITAS NORVIC on the reverse.

HALFGROAT

Both heavy and light issues have on their obverse:
EDWARD DI GRA REX ANGL Z FRAN

The reverse reads: **POSUI DEUM ADIUTOREM MEUM**

All heavy halfgroats (1461-1464) have: **CIVITAS LONDON** because only the London mint operated during those years, but there were several heavy issues with different privy and other marks including lis, pellet, crescent, quatrefoil, trefoil and annulet.

Light halfgroats (1464-1470) were struck at London, Bristol, Coventry, Norwich, York and Canterbury, so reverse legend might have: **CIVITAS LONDON, VILLA BRISTOW (or BRESTOW), CIVITAS COVETRE, CIVITAS NORWIC (or NORVIC), CIVITAS EBORACI or CIVITAS CANTOR**

Again a variety of privy marks were used on the light halfgroats. Additionally, Canterbury halfgroats have a knot below the king's bust. York halfgroats have quatrefoils by the king's neck.

Canterbury halfgroat   York halfgroat

PENNY

Both heavy and light issues have on their obverse:
EDWARD DI GRA REX ANGL
Five mints issued pennies: London, Durham, Bristol, Canterbury and York. Privy marks included lis, pellet, quatrefoil, annulet, trefoil, mascle, as well as various crosses and letters.

The Yorkists - Edward IV

For example, the BRISTOL mint may have: **VILLA BRISTOW** or **VILLA BRISTOLL**, with quatrefoils or saltire crosses by the king's neck ... or a trefoil to right of the neck.

Bristol penny with trefoil to right of neck

DURHAM pennies may have:
CIVITAS DUNOLM, CIVITAS DVNOLI or CIVITAS DER[H]AM.
Some have a rose at the centre of the reverse cross ... while others have a letter D (reversed) and a quatrefoil by the king's neck.

Two Durham pennies with different privy marks and lettering

RICHARD III 1483-1485

The last Yorkist king was born Richard of Gloucester, uncle to the young Edward V, who disappeared with his infant brother while under the ambitious Richard's supposed protection.

War banner

Before usurping the crown, Richard had a strong power base in the north, and his reliance on northerners during his reign was to increase resentment in the south. Yet on becoming king, he attempted genuine reconciliation with those Lancastrians purged from office by Edward IV; but the suspicion of murder hung heavily about him.

Mint mark

When Henry Tudor, direct descendant of John of Gaunt, landed at Milford Haven to claim the throne, Richard III, with a much larger army marching beneath his wild boar banner, met him at Bosworth, Leicestershire. The Tudors won the day, killing Richard III, who they buried without a monument in Leicester. During the reign of Henry VIII his bones were dug up and scattered.

ENGLANDS' STRIKING HISTORY

The Yorkists - Richard III

Desperate for popular acceptance as king, he used as a mint mark the heraldic emblem already associated with his title, Duke of Gloucester. The wild boar's head can be seen on the obverse of many of his pennies, which have: **RICARD DEI GRA REX ANG(L)**
They were minted at London, York and Durham.

Durham penny with boar's head mint mark

A groat from the London mint

The other issues of this short reign were **GROATS** and **HALF-GROATS**.

The groats have on obverse:
RICARD DI GRA REX ANGL Z FRANC
They were minted in London and York.

Halfgroats have:
RICARD DI GRA REX ANGLE Z FRA
They were minted only in London.

THE TUDORS: 1485-1603

The red and white Tudor rose symbolizes the union of the two factions cemented by Henry VII's marriage to Elizabeth of York, eldest daughter of Edward IV. The five sovereigns of the Tudor dynasty are among the most well-known figures in regal history: Henry VII, Henry VIII, Edward VI, Mary I and Elizabeth I. They ruled for 118 eventful years, during which England became a leading colonial power, breeding men such as Raleigh, Drake and Frobisher. At home commerce and trade expanded, London grew, consumerism flourished, the need for coinage increased at all social levels.

The Tudor court nurtured Shakespeare, Marlowe, Spenser and Wolsey. But the Tudor decades also witnessed two changes of official religion, resulting in the martyrdom of many innocent believers, both Protestant and Roman Catholic. The fear of Roman Catholicism induced by the Reformation was to last for several centuries and to play an influential role in the succession.

HENRY VII: 1485-1509

After defeating Richard III the new king set about securing his hold on the throne by ousting every member of the aristocracy who had supported the Yorkist cause; but rather than surrounding himself with powerful Lancastrian sympathizers, Henry VII introduced what became known as the *New Monarchy,* replacing a loose network of semi-independent barons with the firm grip of a monarch capable of imposing his will on peasant and peer alike.

He also imposed heavy customs duties on all imports and exports with a view to filling the royal coffers and thus freeing himself from the need to ask Parliament for funds.

The Tudors - Henry VII

By astute dealings in wool he became immensely rich and spent lavishly on new royal palaces, including Greenwich.

Gold arriving on the Continent from the New World boosted the economies of Spain and the Italian cities, where many newly designed coins were introduced. Henry VII matched them by introducing fresh designs and new denominations in England, making his reign a most interesting one for modern numismatists.

Mintmarks are usually boldly struck on all denominations, so it pays to learn to recognize the main ones for this reign, They include :

Greyhound's head   Scallop   Lis on Sun

Tun   Martlet

The Martlet mintmark can be seen on the obverse and reverse of this groat.

GROAT

Early groats followed the design of the previous reign, with a front-facing monarch's bust, though the crowns on Henry VII issues are tall and often ornate. The obverse legend reads: **HENRIC DI GRA REX ANGL Z FRANC.** The reverse legend reads:
POSVI DEUM ADIVTOREM MEUM

The Tudors - Henry VII

Groats were minted only in London, so the reverse always reads:
CIVITAS LONDON

Note the variety of crowns and mintmarks on these London groats.

HALFGROAT

Early halfgroats differ only slightly from groats in their obverse legend which reads: **HENERIC D[E]I GRA REX ANGL Z FR.** The reverse legend reads: **POSVI DEUM ADIVTOREM MEU[M]**

However, the reverse legend in the centre can differ because halfgroats were struck in London, Canterbury and York: **CIVITAS LONDON, CIVITAS CANTOR or CIVITAS EBORACI**

The Tudors - Henry VII

Halfgroats - Left is Canterbury with letter M at centre of reverse cross (Archbishop Morton). Top is York with keys on obverse (Archbishop Savage). Right is London.

PENNY

Early pennies have the obverse legend: **HENRIC DI GRA REX ANG**

Four mints (London, Canterbury, Durham, York) produced pennies, so reverses differ: **CIVITAS LONDON, CIVITAS CANTOR, CIVITAS DERAM or CIVITAS EBORACI**

Pennies from Canterbury and York shown above. The heavily clipped YORK piece at right can be identified by the quatrefoil at the centre of the rear cross.

HALFPENNY

Halfpennies did not alter greatly throughout the reign. The reverse legend reads:
HENRIC D[E]I GRA REX

Three mints (London, Canterbury, York) produced halfpennies, so reverses differ:
CIVITAS LONDON, CIVITAS CANTOR or CIVITAS EBORACI

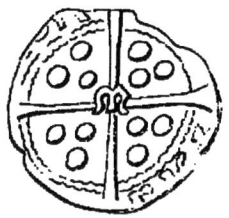

Despite blundered or clipped lettering these halfpennies can be readily identified. The piece at left has a KEY beneath the bust. It is a YORK halfpenny. The piece at right has a letter M at centre reverse. It is a CANTERBURY halfpenny.

FARTHING

Only LONDON struck farthings during this reign. The obverse reads:
HENRIC DI GRA REX

The reverse has: **CIVITAS LONDON**

TESTOON (SHILLING)

The Tudors - Henry VII

Introduced in 1502, the TESTOON's name comes from the Italian *testa* meaning *head*, an obvious reference to the striking profile on the obverse. With a value of 12 pence, its introduction was a reflection on Continent-wide inflation as a result of New World wealth flooding back to Europe. But in England the testoon's arrival aroused little enthusiasm in a country where coin denominations had scarcely altered in more than two hundred years. Testoons remained scarce until the next reign, but small numbers did enter circulation.

Testoons were minted in London, though no mint name appears on the reverse. Obverse legends read:

HENRIC DI GRA REX ANGLIE Z FRAN
or ...... **HENRIC SEPTIM DI GRA REX ANGL Z FRA**
or ...... **HENRIC VII DI GRA REX ANGL Z FRA**

All reverse legends read: **POSUI DEUM ADIVTOE MEU**

PROFILE GROAT

Introduced in 1502, the new groat had greater success than the testoon; it became quite a common coin towards the end of Henry VII's reign.

Obverse legends reads:
HENRIC VII DI GRA REX ANGL Z F
or .... **HENRIC DEI GRA REX ANGLI Z FRA**
or ... **HENRIC SEPTIM DI GRA REX ANGL Z FR**
or ... **HENRIC VII DI GRA REX ANGL Z F**

All reverse legends read: **POSUI DEUM ADIVTOE MEU**

PROFILE HALFGROAT

Profile halfgroats became popular coins after 1502, minted at London, Canterbury and York. Obverse legend reads:

HENRIC VII DI GRA REX AGL Z
or ... **HENRIC DI GRA REX AGL Z**

Reverse reads: **POSVI DEUM ADIVTOREM MEU[M]**

The Tudors - Henry VII

Halfgroats - Keys beneath the reverse shield on the left indicate the YORK mint.

SOVEREIGN PENNY

Introduced towards the end of Henry VII's reign, these attractive silver coins followed the style of the contemporary gold sovereign, depicting on the obverse the king sitting on his throne. The reverse followed the style of the PROFILE GROAT, depicting a shield and cross.
Obverse legends read: **HENRICUS DI GRA REX ANG**

Three mints produced sovereign pennies, so reverse legends read:
CIVITAS LONDON, CIVITAS DERHAM[DURHAM] or CIVITAS EBORACI

A Sovereign penny from York. Two Durham examples are shown on the previous page.

NOTE: No sovereign halfpennies or farthings were minted because those coins were regarded as too small for the design.

ENGLANDS' STRIKING HISTORY

HENRY VIII 1509-1547

Numismatists regard Henry VIII's outrages against England's currency as no less shocking than the treatment of his wives (two beheaded, two divorced, one died in childbirth, one outlived him). When he came to the throne he inherited a huge family fortune, later supplemented by sales of monastic lands and a habit of borrowing money then threatening retribution against anyone who asked for repayment. Nevertheless, he debased the coinage ruthlessly to pay for his extravagant lifestyle and unsuccessful wars. Shortly before his death silver coins became so adulterated they altered colour in circulation and earned the king his *Old Coppernose* nickname.

The Tudor dynasty had been established by conquest. Henry VIII, its second monarch, desperately needed heirs. Yet his six marriages produced only one sickly son and an insecure succession with two princesses (Mary and Elizabeth, who at one stage had been declared illegitimate), none of whom were to have children. His legacy included dangerous Protestant-Roman Catholic differences within the kingdom. Among his few lasting memorials we can list some luxurious palaces and a greatly enlarged navy.

TESTOON

Striking portraits and Tudor rose reverses make these coins interesting to modern collectors, though at the time of their issue - late in Henry VIII's reign - most "silver" money contained up to two-thirds copper. The obverse legends on testoons minted in London (Tower Mint) read:

HENRIC VIII DG AGL FR Z HIB REX
or ... **HENRIC 8 DG AGL FR Z HIB REX**

Reverses have: **POSUI DEUM ADIVTOREM MEUM**

Historic Coinage

www.HistoricCoinage.com

Coins from the heart of historic England
Hammered coins bought & sold

Historic Coinage
Email: Clive@HistoricCoinage.com
Post: Clive Knipe, PO Box 90, Virginia Water
Surrey, GU25 9AQ, England

A second London mint (SOUTHWARK) also produced testoons. They can be distinguished from TOWER MINT coins by their reverse legend:
CIVITAS LONDON
A third mint (BRISTOL) has the reverse:
CIVITAS BRISTOLLIE

Testoons from TOWER (above) and SOUTHWARK (right) mints.

GROAT

His earliest groats simply altered HENRIC VII to HENRIC VIII in their obverse legends, even retaining the previous monarch's portrait. But a youthful Henry VIII image was used for the second coinage of 1526-1544 minted in London and York. All have the obverse legend: **HENRIC VIII DI GRA REX AGL A FRA**

London's reverse reads: **POSVI DEU ADIVTORE MEU**

York's reverse has: **CIVITAS EBORACI**

Two exceptions were groats from Tournai, France, where Henry VIII maintained an English mint up to 1526. The reverse reads:
CIVITAS TORNACEN
... and ....
groats minted in London for use in Ireland. They have the obverse legend:
HENRIC 8 DI GRA HIB REX AGL Z F
(HENRY VIII BY THE GRACE OF GOD KING OF IRELAND ENGLAND AND FRANCE)

The Tudors - Henry VIII

The third coinage (1544-1547), together with posthumous groats issued 1547-1551, all have the obverse legend:
HENRIC 8 D G AGL FRA Z HIB REX

Six mints issued these base silver coins, by now extremely dull in colour, and all depicted an ageing king. Reverses:

                POSVI DEUM ADIVTORE MEU (TOWER)
                CIVITAS LONDON (SOUTHWARK)
                CIVITAS BRISTOLI (BRISTOL)
                CIVITAS CANTOR (CANTERBURY)
                CIVITAS EBORACI (YORK)
... and ...   **REDDE CVIQUE QVOD SVVM EST**
      (DURHAM HOUSE, which translates as: Render to each that which is his own)

Note: Durham House was a London property belonging to Durham Cathedral. It had been used as a mint for ecclesiastic issues, but was sequestrated by the king.

Groats from the Tower, York, Canterbury, Durham House and Southwark mints (starting top left, working from left to right).

ENGLANDS' STRIKING HISTORY

HALFGROAT

Halfgroats from Durham House and Bristol mints.

From 1509-1526 halfgroats carried the previous monarch's portrait with the legend altered to read HENRIC VIII. All had the obverse legend: **HENRIC VIII DI GRA REX AGL Z**

Reverse legends for the four mints that issued halfgroats were:
POSVI DEV ADIVTOE MEV (London)
CIVITAS CANTOR (Canterbury) with **W.A.** (Archbishop Warham) next to the shield.
POSVI DEV ADIVTOE MEU (York) with **X.B.** or **T.W.** and/or keys and/or a cardinal's hat next to the shield.
CIVITAS TORNACEN (Tournai)

The second coinage (1526-1544) showed a youthful Henry VIII. These halfgroats were struck at London, Canterbury and York. Obverse legends were:
HENRIC VIII D. GR REX AGL Z FR (London)
HENRIC D.G. AGL Z HIB REX (London)
HENRIC VIII D GR AGL Z FR (Canterbury)
HENRIC VIII D GR AGL Z FR (York)

Reverse legends for the three mints that issued halfgroats were:

POSVI DEV ADIVTOE MEU (London)

PENNY

Between 1509-1526 his pennies were sovereign types showing Henry VIII on his throne, with a shield-and-cross reverse and the mint named in the legend.
Obverse legend on all reads: **HENRIC DI GRA REX ANGLE**
The reverse reads:
CIVITAS LONDON, CIVITAS CANTOR or CIVITAS DVRRAM

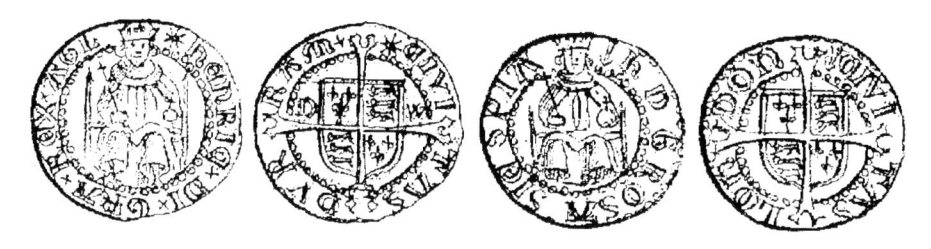

Sovereign pennies from Durham and London.

Between 1526-1544 the obverse legend became the latin for "Henry by the grace of god, a rose without a thorn:

H. D. G. ROSA SIE SPIA

Reverses remained largely unaltered, but the mints were now:
(CIVITAS) LONDON, CANTOR, DURRAM and **EBORACI.**

Between 1544-1547 and posthumously between 1547-1551 debased silver coins depicting a much older, bearded, front-facing bust were issued. The obverse legend read:

H. D. G. ROSA SINE SPINA

Reverses retained the cross-and-shield design, with mints named as:

CIVITAS LONDON, CIVITAS BRISTOLI, CIVITAS EBORACI and **CIVITAS CANTOR**

The DURHAM HOUSE mint in London differed with a reverse reading:
RED CUIQ Q S EST (RENDER TO EACH THAT WHICH IS HIS OWN)

HALFPENNY

Four mints struck halfpence during this reign: London, Canterbury, York and Bristol. Between 1509-1526 the obverse legend reads: **HENRIC DI GRA REX AGL**

with mint names on reverses:

CIVITAS LONDON ... CIVITAS CANTOR

Between 1526-1544 the obverse legend reads:

H DG ROSA SIE SPIA

with mint names on reverses: **CIVITAS LONDON ... CIVITAS CANTOR ... CIVITAS EBORACI**

Between 1544-1547, and posthumously between 1547-1551 the obverse legend reads:
H . D.G . ROSA SINE SPINA
with mint names on reverses:

CIVITAS LONDON ... CIVITAS CANTOR ... CIVITAS EBORACI ... CIVITAS BRISTOLI

FARTHING

A few extremely rare farthings are known for this reign. Obverse legends usually read: **RUTILANS ROSA** (A DAZZLING ROSE)

Reverses usually have: **DEO GRACIA or DEO GRACIS** (BY GOD'S GRACE)

EDWARD VI 1547-1553

King at ten and dead at sixteen, the only son of Henry VIII had little opportunity to stamp Tudor authority on a nation that began to fragment in a power struggle between Protestants and Roman Catholics the moment the old king passed away. A staunch supporter of his father's Reformation, the sickly juvenile could do little to prevent Catholic Mary grabbing the crown.

Towards the end of his short reign attempts were made to restore public faith in the country's coinage. Innovations included the introduction of four new denominations, and a return to high grade silver. But not before standards sank so low that base pennies passed as halfpence, and base halfpence were accepted only as farthings.

CROWN:

This fine silver issue (image above is actual size) came late in the reign as part of a move back to the sterling silver of earlier centuries. It portrays a dashing figure of the young king on horseback with - innovatively - the date in numerals beneath. Extremely popular at the time of issue, this coin attracts modern collectors as the first English coin dated in numerals. Dates include 1551, 1552 and 1553. The obverse legend reads:
EDWARD VI DG. AGL FRANC Z HIBER REX
(EDWARD VI BY THE GRACE OF GOD KING OF ENGLAND,

The reverse shows the royal arms, a cross and the legend:
POSUI DEUM ADIVTORE MEU

HALFCROWN:

These interesting coins were introduced late in the reign as an alternative to gold halfcrowns which often became lost because they were so small. They proved even more popular than the silver crown. Three different portraits on the king on horseback were used, two show a walking horse; one has a galloper. Dates, which appear on the obverse, include 1551, 1552 and 1553.

The Tudors - Edward VI

Obverse legend reads:

EDWARD VI DG AGL FRA Z HIB REX

The reverse has:

POSUI DEUM ADIVITORE MEUM

SHILLING:

Early in the reign the shilling was no more than the testoon by another name. The first issues continued the debasing practices of the previous monarch. They show a right-facing crowned profile of the young king. Some shillings include the date in Roman numerals within their legends. An oval shield flanked by the initials **E R** appears on most reverses.

Dated *Undated*

Usually the obverse legends read: **TIMOR DOMINI FONS VITE,** which translates to: FEAR OF THE LORD IS THE FOUNTAIN OF LIFE.

The reverse usually reads: **EDWARD VI DG AGL FRA Z HIB REX.** On a few rare coins obverse and reverse legends were transposed.

If dated the Latin numerals will read:
MDXLVIII (1548) ... **MDXLIX** (1549)... **MDL** (1550)... **MDLI**

The Tudors - Edward VI

The Durham House mint struck undated debased shillings with the reverse reading:

INIMICOS EIUS UNDUAM CONFUSIONE
AS FOR HIS ENEMIES I SHALL CLOTHE THEM WITH SHAME

Between 1551-1553 high grade silver shillings struck at the Tower mint achieved widespread popularity. They had a new obverse portrait of the young king flanked by a Tudor rose and the coins value (**XII**) expressed in pence. The obverse legend read:
EDWARD VI DG AGL. FRA A HIB REX
The reverse legend reverted to the old
POSUI DEU ADIUTORE MEUM
while the coin's reverse had the royal shield and a cross.

The new shilling of 1551-1553 with its fine portrait of Edward VI

SIXPENCE:

Because so much bad silver money had been issued in the decades before 1551 the new sixpence in fine silver proved an immediate success, so much so that London and York mints were required to meet extra demand.

Obverse legend reads:
EDWARD VI DG AGL FRA Z HIB REX
with a Tudor rose to the left and the value (**VI**) in Roman numerals to the right.

York 6d

The London reverse has:
POSUI DEUM ADIVTOREM MEUM

York strikings have: **CIVITAS EBORACI**

THREEPENCE:

Perhaps because of the unfamiliarity of odd-numbered denominations (apart from the penny) the public did not accept the innovative three-penny piece. People had become accustomed to dealing in groats and half-groats. This coin was not issued again until Elizabeth I's reign.

York 3d

Obverse legend and the denomination (**III**) differ from the sixpence. The obverse legend reads:
EDWARD VI DG ANG FRA Z HIB REX
London reverse has: **POSUI DEUM ADIUTOREM MEUM**

GROAT:

Very few groats were struck during this reign, in part because huge numbers of low grade groats from the previous reign still circulated; also because later in the reign it was expected that the sixpence and threepence would render the groat obsolete. But the public seemed to prefer groats, despite their dull and often chipped appearance.

The Tudors - Edward VI

The few legible pieces bearing Edward VI's profile have an obverse legend that includes: **EDWARD 6** ... or ... **EDWARD D.G.** ... or (rarely) **EDOARD 6**

The reverse has a royal shield and cross, sometimes with: **CIVITAS LONDON** or with part of: **POSVI DEUM ADIVTOREM MEUM**

HALFGROAT:

Very few halfgroats were struck during this reign for the reasons already given under GROAT. The obverse portrait and the royal shield and cross reverse are similar to the groat. Three mints produced the few Edward VI halfgroats that were minted: Reverse legends read:

POSVI (etc) for TOWER ... **CIVITAS LONDON** for SOUTHWARK ... **CIVITAS CANTOR** for CANTERBURY

PENNY:

Vast quantities of silver poured into Europe in the mid-16th century when, despite the ravages of wars, the general standard of living rose. In England increased wealth reflected in increased use of coins such as groats and shillings. The standard penny gradually became less important in the marketplace.

In consequence Edward VI's mints struck very few, and almost all of them at the beginning of the reign when base coinage circulated widely. A rare unworn specimen is depicted here:

... with two worn specimens shown on the next page, the first at actual size:

The obverse has a central Tudor rose and:
E D G ROSA SINE SPINA
The reverse has a shield and cross with:
CIVITAS LONDON

The Tudors - Edward VI

A few Sovereign pennies were struck in fine silver in 1551-1553. As shown here, the legends read: **E. D. G. ROSA SINE SPINA**, with **CIVITAS LONDON** on the reverse.

HALFPENNY AND FARTHING

Numerous base pennies circulated as halfpence and farthings, each value determined by how dark the metal as a result of its copper content, and how much the coin had cracked around its brittle edges.

A few base silver halfpennies were struck in 1547-1549 bearing the profile bust of Edward VI and: **EDG ROSA SIN SPIN** on the obverse, and with a long cross and pellets design on the reverse with the legend: **CIVITAS LONDON** ... or .... **CIVITAS BRISTOLI**

A tiny farthing with a portcullis obverse and cross with pellets reverse (as below) was struck in base silver late in the reign. The obverse legend reads: **E. D. G. ROSA SINE SPI**
The reverse has: **CIVITAS LONDON**

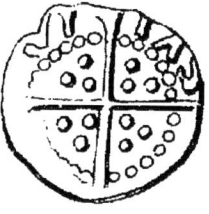

MARY, and PHILIP & MARY: 1553-1558

Better known to us as *Bloody Mary*, she was the sole surviving child of Henry VIII's marriage to Katherine of Aragon. When the young king Edward VI (her half-brother) died unexpectedly in 1553 Mary publicly claimed the English crown and called upon Roman Catholics to muster at Framlington Castle in Norfolk before marching on London. Bloodiness soon followed. Several hundred burnings-at-the-stake and beheadings of anti-papists led quickly to the restoration of Catholicism and the redecoration of parish churches. Mary sought a marriage with the devoutly Catholic Philip of Spain. She desperately wanted an heir who would prevent the accession of Elizabeth. Unfortunately for Mary her several claims to be an expectant mother proved false alarms and Philip abandoned her. In 1558 Calais - England's last French possession - fell to a French siege. A few weeks later an influenza epidemic swept across England. One-fifth of the population died, including Mary. Her enemies called her misfortunes divine retribution. They soon demanded that a Protestant should once again take the crown.

PENNY:

During her sole monarch years (1553-1554) Mary issued base and fine silver pennies, the base circulating as halfpence. On both issues the obverse legend reads: **M.D.G. ROSA SINE SPINA** with the reverse on most of the fine silver reading: **VERITAS TEMP FILIA** (TRUTH IS THE DAUGHTER OF TIME). The base issues have reverses reading: **CIVITAS LONDON**

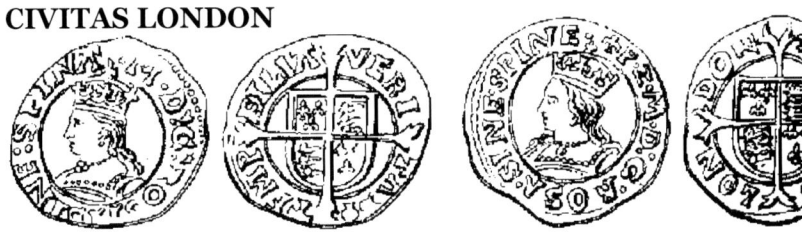

The Tudors - Mary, Philip & Mary

When Philip of Spain became king consort (1554-1558) the obverse legend on pennies altered to:
P Z M D G ROSA SINE SPINE (PHILIP AND MARY BY THE GRACE OF GOD A ROSE WITHOUT A THORN). The reverse was:
CIVITAS LONDON

Fine and base silver issues of these pennies were struck, the base serving as halfpence.

GROAT AND HALFGROAT:

Obverse legend reads: **MARIA D G ANG FRA Z HIB REGI** (MARY BY THE GRACE OF GOD QUEEN OF ENGLAND, FRANCE, IRELAND)

Reverse reads: **VERITAS TEMPORIS FILIA** (TRUTH IS THE DAUGHTER OF TIME)

Large numbers of Groats were struck during Mary's sole reign. Halfgroats, identical in all but size, are much rarer.

The obverse type used for the groat and halfgroat.

SHILLING

To publicly confirm Philip of Spain's status as joint monarch in England fine silver shillings depicting him alongside his queen were issued from 1554-1558. Both their Spanish titles and their English titles were announced on coins with differing legends, though all were struck at the Tower mint.

The obverse legend on shillings giving their Spanish title read:

PHILIP ET MARIA DG R ANG FR NEAP PR HISP
(PHILIP AND MARY BY THE GRACE OF GOD KING AND QUEEN OF ENGLAND FRANCE AND NAPLES. PRINCE AND PRINCESS OF SPAIN)

The reverse reads:
POSUIMUS DEUM ADIUTOREM NOSTRUM

Shillings with the English title have the obverse legend:
PHILIP ET MARIA DG REX ET REGINA ANGL
(PHILIP AND MARY BY THE GRACE OF GOD KING AND QUEEN OF THE ENGLISH)

Both were struck with or without dates and values in Roman numerals (**XII**).

A dated shilling with value on reverse and Spanish titles.

SIXPENCE

The SIXPENCE was struck with Spanish and English titles. On the Spanish, the obverse reads:

PHILIP ET MARIA D G R ANG FR NEAP PR HISP (PHILIP AND MARY BY THE GRACE OF GOD KING AND QUEEN OF ENGLAND FRANCE AND NAPLES. PRINCE AND PRINCESS OF SPAIN)

The reverse reads: **POSUIMUS DEUM ADIUTOREM NOSTRUM**

Shillings with the English title have the obverse legend:
PHILIP ET MARIA DG REX ET REGINA AN
(PHILIP AND MARY BY THE GRACE OF GOD KING AND QUEEN OF THE ENGLISH)

Both were struck with and without DATES and values in Roman numerals (**VI**).

Sixpences with Spanish and English titles

ELIZABETH I: 1558-1603

The last Tudor monarch was the daughter of Henry VIII and Anne Boleyn. Intelligent, educated (she spoke six languages), determined, shrewd; her 45-year reign is generally considered one of the most glorious in English history, thanks in part to Elizabeth's astute political judgement and her choice of ministers. The Elizabethan years were a time of colonisation and trade expansion, with plantations in the Americas, and the establishment of the East India Company in Asia. However, Elizabeth's reign also witnessed threats of invasion from Spain and from France. Costly wars caused inflation and severe economic depression long after the defeat of the Spanish Armada. Nevertheless, Elizabeth I became a legend in her lifetime, revered by the general public as their *Virgin Queen*.

HALFPENNY

Because large numbers of base metal coins from previous reigns continued to circulate as low denomination money, no farthings were minted, nor were any new halfpence needed until more than twenty years of Elizabeth I's reign had elapsed. In the early 1580's inflation had pushed the value of silver so high that only very small coins could be struck as halfpence. They carried no portrait of the monarch and no legends; instead the obverse had the royal portcullis, while the reverse had a long cross and pellets.

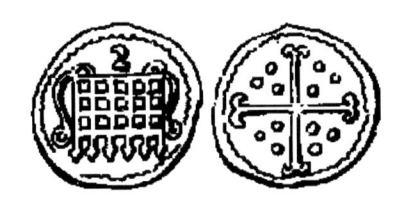

The Tudors - Elizabeth I

THREE-FARTHINGS

This small silver coin has a bust of the queen with a rose behind on its obverse. The obverse legend reads: **E.D.G. ROSA SINE SPINA**. The reverse reads: **CIVITAS LONDON ...** with a **DATE** over the shield:

PENNY

Pennies were struck throughout Elizabeth I's entire reign. They varied little during those forty-five years, depicting a relatively young queen on the obverse and a shield with cross on the reverse. The penny has NO ROSE behind the monarch's head ... and *usually* NO DATE.
The obverse legend reads: **E.D.G. ROSA SINE SPINA**
The reverse reads: **CIVITAS LONDON**

A rare penny variety (depicted below) carried the date **1558** within the obverse legend.

THREE-HALFPENCE

Confusingly for modern collectors looking at clipped Elizabethan coins, this denomination differs only in size from the THREE-FARTHINGS. Unclipped the three-halfpenny piece measures 16-17 mm, while the three-farthings measures 14 mm. (The three-pence coin - very similar in appearance - is much larger at 19-21 mm.)

The Tudors - Elizabeth I

HALFGROAT

Although the pictorial elements on the halfgroat - monarch's bust, shield, cross - are very similar to the penny, most halfgroats carry different legends. The obverse reads: **ELIZABETH D.G. ANG FRA Z HIB REG** or ... **ELIZABETH D.G. ANG FRA ET HIB REGINA**
The reverse reads: **POSUI DEU ADIVTOREM MEU**

Some late varieties (1582-1602) have legends identical to those on the penny; however, they can be distinguished by TWO PELLETS (for 2d) behind the monarch's head.

Late halfgroat with TWO PELLETS behind the bust.

TWOPENCE-FARTHING

This unusual denomination resulted from Elizabeth I's decision to return to the fine silver standards of the centuries prior to her father's reign. She decreed that base silver shillings issued during the reign of her half-brother, Edward VI, should be called in, countermarked with a ROYAL PORTCULLIS, then reissued with a face value equal to their true silver content. That amount was twopence-farthing.

The original coins were invariably badly worn and dark in colour; it is the condition of the countermark that determines the coin's value as a collector's piece.

THREEPENCE

This denomination was minted as a hammered coin during the years 1561 and 1582. Although very similar to the halfgroat in size, and despite its identical legends, bust, shield and cross, it has a ROSE behind the monarch's head, and it also carries a date on the reverse. So, too, do the three-farthing and three-halfpenny issues, but the three-penny piece is somewhat bigger.

The obverse legend reads: **ELIZABETH D G. ANG FR ET HIB REGINA**. The reverse has: **POSUI DEU ADIUTOREM MEU**

GROAT

This denomination appeared for only a few years (1559-1561), probably because adequate supplies of other small silver denominations satisfied demand. Groats have NO DATE and NO ROSE.

Obverse legend reads: **ELIZABETH D G ANG FRA Z HIB REGI** or ... **ELIZABETH D G ANG FRA ET HIB REGINA**

Reverse reads: **POSUI DEU ADIUTOREM MEU**

FOURPENCE-HALFPENNY

As with the twopence-farthing, this unusual denomination resulted from Elizabeth I's decision to return to the fine silver standards of the centuries prior to her father's reign. She decreed that base silver shillings issued during the reign of her half-brother, Edward VI, should be called in, countermarked with a SEATED GREYHOUND, then re-issued with a face value equal to their true silver content. That amount was fourpence-halfpenny. The original coins are invariably badly worn and dark in colour; it is the condition of the countermark that determines the coin's value as a collector's piece.

SIXPENCE

Enormous numbers of sixpences appeared between 1561-1602. This coin, like the THREEPENCE, almost always has a ROSE behind the monarch's portrait and a DATE above the rear shield; but the unclipped SIXPENCE has a diameter of 26-27 mm compared to the 19-21mm of the unclipped threepence. The obverse legend reads:
ELIZABETH DG. ANG FRA ET HIB REGINA
or ... **ELIZAB D G ANG FR ET HIB REGI**
The reverse has: **POSUI DEU ADIVTOREM MEU**

SHILLING

An unclipped Elizabeth I shilling has a diameter of more than 30 mm, so although it has NO DATE and NO ROSE, it cannot be confused with the GROAT, at under 25 mm, even though their legends are also very similar. On the shilling the obverse reads:

	ELIZABET(H) DG ANG FRA(N) Z HIB REGINA
or ...	**ELIZABETH DG ANG FRA ET HIB REGINA**
or ...	**ELIZAB DG ANG FR ET HIB REGI**

The reverse has:

	POSUI DEUM ADIVTOREM MEUM
or ...	**POSUI DEU ADIUTOREM MEU(M)**

HALFCROWN

In 1601-1602 silver halfcrowns almost 35 mm in diameter were struck, reflecting the vast flood of bullion coming to Europe from the New World. These coins bear a superb portrait of Elizabeth I holding a sceptre. The obverse legend reads:
ELIZABETH D.G ANG FRA ET HIBER REGINA
The reverse has: **POSUI DEUM ADIUTOREM MEUM**

CROWN

This coin, identical in legend to the HALFCROWN, has a diameter of more than 40 mm. Like the halfcrown, it was struck between 1601-1602 and proved a very popular issue.

NOTE: *Milled coinage produced with a horse-driven machine, were minted in this reign. Denominations include the silver shilling, sixpence, groat, threepence, halfgroat and three-farthings. As non-hammered coins, they fall outside the scope of this book.*

The Stuarts:

1603 to the End of Hammered Coinage

They began as medieval royal stewards (= land agents for Norman barons who seized most of the best land in Scotland after 1066) and changed the Scottish spelling of their name (Stewart) to the French version (Stuart) when Mary I was exiled in Paris.

The failed Gunpowder Plot ... the lost Civil War ... the terrors of the Great Plague ... the destructions of the Fire of London .... the defeat of Bonnie Prince Charlie. Just a sample of the numerous blunders and disasters that befell their house until it finally collapsed after all of Queen Anne's eighteen children died and the crown passed to the House of Hanover. The Stuarts who concern us here - James the First, Charles the First and Charles the Second - suffered consistent misfortune, despite their glamour and occasional brilliance.

JAMES I: 1603-1625

James was Elizabeth I's nearest royal relative. Both were directly descended from Henry VII, the first Tudor king. In 1603 Elizabeth died childless and James inherited the throne of England. He moved south immediately and at once began to impose heavy taxes in efforts to raise money for an army to secure his hold on the crown. All Stuarts believed passionately that they possessed a divine right to rule. They bitterly resented any interference from Parliament. James soon resorted to selling knighthoods and monopolies, including the lucrative private monopoly of minting copper farthings, with sixty percent of the profits going to the king. When he died in 1625, James I was not greatly mourned.

CROWN

With its striking portrait of the king on horseback, the crown proved a popular coin throughout the reign, though more for its convenience to merchants and the middle classes than for the king's popularity. Crowns struck during the first year of the reign have the obverse legend:
IACOBUS DG ANG SCO FRAN ET HIBER REX
(JAMES BY THE GRACE OF GOD KING OF ENGLAND SCOTLAND FRANCE AND IRELAND)

The reverse reads:
EXURGAT DEUS DISSIPENTUR INIMICI

(Actual Size)

Crowns struck after 1604 have the obverse legend:
IACOBUS DG MAG BRIT FRAN ET HIB REX
(JAMES BY THE GRACE OF GOD KING OF GREAT BRITAIN FRANCE AND IRELAND)
The reverse reads: QUAE DEUS CONIUNXIT NEMO SEPARET
   (WHAT GOD HATH JOINED LET NO MAN PUT ASUNDER)

NOTE: Any crown depicting a shield with a plume above the reverse crown (as here) was struck from silver obtained from the Royal Mines in Wales

The Stuarts - James I

HALFCROWN

Although approximately 10mm smaller in diameter than the CROWN, this coin is almost identical in its portraits and legends. On early issues the obverse legend has minor differences and reads:
IACOBUS D.G. ANG SCO FRAN ET HIB REX
The reverse reads: **EXURGAT DEUS DISSIPENTUR INIMICI**
Later issues have identical legends to those on crowns.

SHILLING

All shillings have the denomination in roman numerals **(XII)** behind the king's head on the obverse. The reverse has a royal shield. The obverse legend reads:

IACOBUS DG. ANG SCO FRA ET HIB REX

From 1604 it became:
IACOBUS MAG BRI(T) FRA ET HIB REX
Reverse legends imitate those described under CROWN and HALFCROWN.

SIXPENCE

With identical obverse and reverse legends to the SHILLING, this coin might be confused with a clipped shilling. Fortunately all sixpences have their denomination in roman numerals **(VI)** behind the king's head. Additionally - and unlike the shilling - sixpences have their date in arabic numerals **(1605)**, etc. above the reverse shield.

The Stuarts - James I

A Sixpence

HALFGROAT: The first coinage of this reign (1603-1604) had a halfgroat bearing the king's crowned head with the denomination **(II)** behind, and the obverse legend: **I.D.G. ROSA SINE SPINA**. The reverse of this coin carried a shield, but no legend.

The second and third coinages (1604-1625) had a halfgroat depicting a crowned rose on its obverse, and a crowned thistle on the reverse. The obverse legend was identical to the first coinage. The reverse carried a political message:

TUEATUR UNITA DEUS
(MAY GOD GUARD THESE UNITED KINGDOMS)

PENNY

The earliest penny differs from the earliest halfgroat only in having the denomination **(I)** behind the king's head. The later ROSE and THISTLE issue has NO CROWN above rose or thistle. Its obverse and reverse legends are identical to those on the halfgroat.

The Stuarts - James I, Charles I

HALFPENNY

Although they have neither obverse nor reverse legends, the halfpennies of James I have very distinctive designs. The 1603 - 1604 issue has a PORTCULLIS. The reverse has a LONG CROSS with 3 pellets in each segment. The later issues (1604 - 1625) have a ROSE obverse, and a THISTLE reverse.

CHARLES I : 1625-1649

Charles Stuart believed God had appointed him king, and that divine will should brook no interference from Parliament. Worse still, just after his coronation he married Henrietta of France, a Catholic, and made her queen of England. Those events occurred at a time when England had no external enemies threatening invasion; Englishmen had begun to look upon Parliament as a place where they could achieve civil liberties and rights. Charles wanted none of those things for his subjects, so he refused to open Parliament for eleven years.

In 1639 he ran out of cash and had to call both houses to session to pass new tax laws. The Commons not only refused to vote him royal funds; they also refused to end their session. Inevitably Civil War followed in 1640. Parliamentary forces, helped by the Scottish Army, finally defeated the Royalists at Naseby 1645. The king surrendered and became a prisoner. But in 1649, following a bungled attempt by Royalists to regain power, Charles I was tried and executed.

The Stuarts - Charles I

POUND

During the Civil War, Charles struck money to pay his army at several cities and towns. The silver pound, minted at Oxford and Shrewsbury, has its denomination and date on the reverse: roman numerals **(XX)** for twenty shillings; dates: 1642 (Shrewsbury) 1642, 1643, 1644 (Oxford). The obverse shows the king, sword in hand, on his charger. Some pounds depict the enemy's armour and weapons trampled underfoot. The obverse legend reads: **CAROLUS D G MAG BRIT FRA ET HIB[ER] REX** (Charles by the grace of god king of Great Britain France and Ireland). The reverse has: **EXURGAT DEUS DISSIPENTUR INIMICI RELIG PROT LEG ANGL LIBER PAR** (Let god arise and his enemies be scattered the religion of the protestants the laws of England the liberty of parliament).

HALFPOUND

Almost identical in all but size (the full Pound is over 5cm in diameter) and its reverse denomination **(X)** denoting ten shillings, the silver halfpound was struck at Oxford and Shrewsbury from 1642 - 1643. Obverse and reverse legends are as for the POUND.

CROWN

When Charles I controlled London's Tower Mint (1625 - 1642) he struck crowns depicting himself on horseback with sword aloft, and with the royal arms on the reverse. Obverse legend reads: **CAROLUS DG MAG BRIT FRA ET HIB REX.** The reverse reads: **CHRISTO AUSPICE REGNO** (I reign under Christ's Auspices)

Crowns with identical legends and a variety of mounted kings were struck by the Parliamentarians after Charles left London.

In the provinces, Civil War crowns were struck at Oxford, Shrewsbury, Exeter and Truro. Some are dated (1642-1645); some state their value with a roman numeral **(V)** on the reverse. Most retained legends very close to the Tower Mint issues, though reverses on Oxford and Shrewsbury crowns had the more belligerent : **EXURGAT DEUS DISSIPENTUR INIMICI** (Let god arise and my enemies be scattered). With the usual legend in the centre: **RELIG PROT LEG ANGL LIBER PAR**

A rare siege coin from Scarborough is shown below right. This was the only Crown siege piece. Seige pieces were made from odd shaped bits of silver plate. It depicts Scarborough Castle, with **S** for the town, and with a roman numeral, **V** for five shillings.

Note: A milled silver crown was produced by the London Mint between 1631 - 1639.

HALFCROWN

During Charles I's tumultuous reign, halfcrowns were struck in London and in Aberystwyth, York, Hereford, Shrewsbury, Oxford, Bristol, Truro, Exeter, Hartlebury and Chester - as well as in Newark and Scarborough as siege pieces. Inevitably there are numerous varieties; but beginners should note the following points:

Although no denomination appears on halfcrowns (apart from on siege pieces), they are the smallest coins of this reign to depict the king on horseback. Unclipped, a halfcrown's diameter is about 10mm smaller than the approx 44mm Crown.

All but the siege pieces depict the mounted king with raised sword. Obverse and reverse legends are as described in the section on the CROWN. Although the reverse shield appears in many forms, it always carries the royal arms.

This rare Newark siege piece has its value in roman numeral as **XXX** = 30 pence = halfcrown.

SHILLING

Enormous numbers of hammered shillings circulated in England during this reign. Struck by Charles I and by Parliament, all depict the king's head - in more than sixty different styles, not counting minor variations. Often using worn dies, and always working under extreme pressure, the dozen or so mints that produced shillings turned out many very crudely struck specimens. Add the effects of long circulation and much clipping to appreciate why it can be difficult to correctly ascribe a shilling to its mint and year of striking. Nevertheless, beginners can take heart from the fact that all shillings except siege pieces carry a bust of the king. Most have a visible XII next to the bust (= Twelve pence = 1 Shilling).

The Stuarts - Charles I

All shillings, including the siege pieces, carry their denomination in roman numerals **(XII)**. Those with a regal bust have the denomination behind the head. Almost all of the coins have the obverse legend:
CAROLUS DG MAG BRIT FRA ET HIB REX
And the reverse: **CHRISTO AUSPICE REGNO**

The Oxford and Bristol mints were among the very few that managed to squeeze the full DECLARATION legend onto such a small coin.

The Stuarts - Charles I

SIXPENCE

All information given under SHILLING applies to Charles I's sixpences. The only notable differences are that the sixpence is often smaller than the shilling - but beware clipped shillings; and - MOST IMPORTANTLY - the sixpence has its denomination in roman numerals **(VI)** on the obverse, behind the king's bust. The very few siege pieces of this value also use **VI** to denote their value.

GROAT

Neither the king nor Parliament minted groats in London, but during the Civil War, several mints including Aberystwyth, Oxford and Bristol struck them. Irrespective of legends, all groats can be recognized by the roman numerals **IIII** behind the king's bust on the obverse.

The obverse legend reads: **CAROLUS D G M B F ET H REX** (Charles by the grace of god King of Great Britain France and Ireland) or …. **CAROLUS D G MAG BR FRA ET HIB REX** …. with other variations.

The reverse has: **CHRISTO AVSPICE REGNO** or an abbreviated version of the Declaration legend.

THREEPENCE

All information given under GROAT applies to the Charles I's threepence. The only notable differences are that the threepence is often smaller than the groat - but beware clipped groats; and - MOST IMPORTANTLY - the threepence has its denomination in roman numerals **(III)** on the obverse, behind the king's bust.

HALFGROAT

The halfgroat, or two-penny piece, was a most popular coin during this reign. Two main series, with many minor variations, were minted, but the first series - the **CROWNED ROSE ISSUE** - was struck only in London.

Rose Types - the left example shows a Crowned Rose.

The Stuarts - Charles I

The **BUST ISSUE**, minted in London and at provincial mints including Oxford, Aberystwyth, Bristol, Exeter and Worcester, has on its obverse the king's portrait and a version of: **CAROLUS D G M(AG) B F(RA) ET H(IB) REX**

Reverses include a shield, or a plume, or a rose, or part of the Declaration. The reverse outer legend is usually a version of: **IUSTITIA THRONUM FIRMAT**

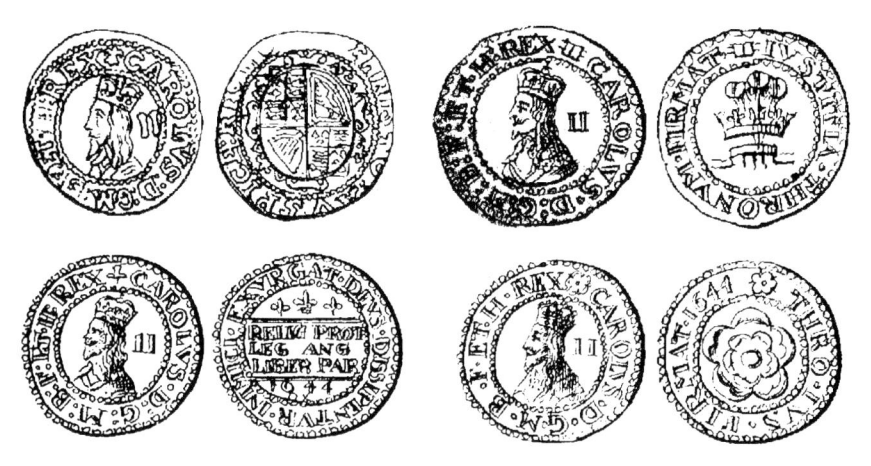

PENNY

During the Civil War most mints struck higher value coins, mainly as pay for troops; but low denominations such as the penny were desperately needed in market-places and taverns as small change. Most pennies came from the Tower Mint before the start of the war. They had an uncrowned rose on obverse and reverse with variations of the legends: **C.D.G. ROSA SINE SPINA IUS THRONUM FIRMAT.**

Other London pennies have the king's bust with a shield reverse. Provincial mints also used the king's bust on pennies, with reverses including plumes, a rose, even one type with part of the Declaration squeezed onto the tiny flan.

Many pennies were clipped, but the denomination as a roman numeral **(I)** can usually be seen on the obverse of the bust types.

The Stuarts - Charles I

Pennies

HALFPENNY

Scarcely any halfpennies were minted during this reign. The Tower Mint produced a two-sided ROSE type without legends. The Aberystwyth mint was the only Royalist source for the piece shown below, which has a rose obverse and a PLUME reverse, again with no legends.

NOTE: *Base metal FARTHINGS were minted during the reign of Charles I; but as this book is primarily concerned with silver coinage they fall outside of our scope here.*

THE COMMONWEALTH 1649-1660

After beheading the king, the Parliamentarians decided to have coins with no monarch's head. The results - shown on this page - were plain and puritanical. All carried a St George shield on the obverse, and another on the reverse, with an Irish shield alongside, space permitting. Apart from the HALFPENNY, all carried a denomination in roman numerals (I, II, VI, XII, IIvi or V) for penny, halfgroat, sixpence, shilling, two-and-sixpence and crown. From SIXPENCE and above they carried dates, and the legends: **THE COMMONWEALTH OF ENGLAND / GOD WITH US**

CHARLES II 1660-1685

When the Protectorship of the Cromwells ended in 1660 the Parliament decided they had suffered enough under the Commonwealth, so they sent to France where Charles II lived in exile. He agreed to the restoration and sailed for England and his coronation. New methods of minting coins, pioneered by Pierre Blondeau and first used with success for the previous portrait issue of Oliver Cromwell coinage (not illustrated in this book) soon superseded hand-striking. By 1663, after over 5000+ years of coins being struck by hand, milled money ousted hammered money forever.

The few hammered coins of the reign all have a crowned king Charles II and usually their value in roman numerals on the obverse **(XXX, XI/XII, VI, IIII, III, II and I)** for halfcrown, shilling, sixpence, fourpence/groat, threepence, twopence and penny. (The earliest coins in the series have no value marked). None were dated. The obverse legend reads: **CAROLUS II DG MAG BRIT F(RAN) ET HIB REX.** The reverse reads: **CHRISTO AUSPICE REGNO.**

The Stuarts - Charles II

Where Do You Go From Here?

This little book serves as no more than a brief introduction to the fascinations of English Hammered Silver Coin Collecting. Within its cover price range it is the very best start on the subject a beginner could make. But a start implies a journey; so where should your next steps take you?

Fifty years ago the answer to that question would undoubtedly have been: "To your local numismatic society." That's where the most experienced collectors in your town congregated at least once a month; all of them with superb VF, even EF collections; most willing to pass on their knowledge to an eager beginner.

In the 21st century, when we have fewer societies and much less time to devote to hobbies of any sort, the next best move for a budding collector is undoubtedly to familiarize yourself with the internet and all it has to offer numismatically.

Just before typing this section I opened a major internet search engine, typed in ENGLISH HAMMERED SILVER COINS and it returned a staggering 177,000 pages. In surfing through the first 100 - all dealers, I found 20 that had high quality illustrated sales lists for viewing on screen. That's a most convenient way to look closely at hammered silver coins, and a good way to familiarize yourself with current market trends.

Using an advanced search facility on a major search engine I was soon viewing museum catalogues, portfolios of private collections, a glossary of numismatic terms, a professional historian's 6,000-word essay on Henry V's money, a medieval coins discussion group's electronic exchanges, a corpus of early medieval hammered silver coin hoards ... and much more. The busiest programme on offer from the most active numismatic society would have trouble providing as much information as was readily available on screen.

Where Do Yoyu Go From Here?

Nevertheless, something important was missing. Surfing the net will pack your head with facts - but we had not handled a single coin during that time. So here's the next piece of advice: Use the internet to surf for details of every up-coming coin fair, and make a determined effort to get to at least one. Don't take a wad of money, but do take a good pocket-sized magnifying glass. (Make a start on your acquisition of useful jargon: advanced collectors call it a loupe.) Pause at every dealer's table where there are English hammered for sale. Cast your eyes fairly rapidly over all the stock and pick out no more than two or three that particularly interest you. ASK the dealer if it's OK to pick up a coin and examine it more closely with your loupe. (Refusals are almost unknown.) With approval obtained, pick up the coin FIRMLY, holding it with a finger and thumb around the edges. To examine the other face turn your hand, don't fumble with the coin. Through the lens your introduction to mintmarks, privy marks, grading, and other aspects of more advanced collecting begins. Ask questions, accept any proffered business cards and printed lists, make pencilled notes for use the next time you surf the internet. A couple of hours spent at a coin fair that has twenty tables devoted to English hammered will gain you the invaluable experience of handling fifty or sixty coins, of looking at them with an ever more critical eye, of listening to knowledgeable dealers talking face-to-face with experienced collectors ... and all for the price of your entrance ticket.

A few months from now you will have outgrown this little book. Don't make the mistake of buying a general catalogue that probably offers not much more that we have given, but with hardback covers. Make the leap to a specialist catalogue, perhaps dealing with one monarch or a single century. It will cost you some tens of pounds ... and that might be a good reason to join your nearest coin club, where there's sure to be an excellent library of borrowable specialist catalogues.

An Alternative Approach:
Find Your Own English Hammered Silver Coins

Throughout the six or seven hundred years covered in this book, you must have noticed the reluctance of most monarchs to issue low denomination coins, especially farthings and halfpennies. The harsh economic facts of a silver coinage based solely on the bullion value of its metal was that low denomination coins were so small they were frequently lost from medieval purses.

Now let's race forward in time to 1971 when decimal coins began to oust the halfcrowns, two-bobs, shillings, tanners, even the already vanishing silver three-penny bits that jangled in our pockets in those days. (Older readers may fondly recall an early Rotographic booklet titled "Check Your Change" that dates from that period). Just before the new coins appeared the Central Statistical Office issued a figure for the numbers of pre-decimal coins that disappeared from circulation every year in Britain throughout the 1960s. It was 180,000,000. One hundred and eighty million pre-decimal coins were lost EVERY YEAR in Britain. Similar losses in proportion to the population had gone on during all previous centuries back to the introduction of coins into our islands by the Celts.

That's why so many people today enjoy, even profit from, the hobby known as metal detecting. If you buy a metal detector (A good one will set you back several hundred pounds) and instead of joining a numismatic society you join a detectorists' club, YOU WILL FIND ENGLISH HAMMERED SILVER COINS. Not sackfuls (though numerous hoards have been discovered by absolute beginners); not pocketfuls (though some very experienced detectorists' finds run to double figures every season); but you will probably have hammered silver coin finds to admire before your first exciting season draws to a close. And your other finds - coppers, trinkets, jewellery, artefacts - can help you recoup your outlay on the machine; perhaps even pay for the purchase of a high-grade hammered silver coin from a dealer.

Most of your detector finds will seem in poor condition when you first recover them from the soil. Some will be so badly corroded they will not merit any numismatic grading. But you will bring up pieces in fair grade ... even in fine ... and now and again in very fine condition.

To Clean or not to Clean? That is the question.

In fact, the question NEVER arises. If you take the numismatic route to coin collecting you don't clean your coins. Full stop.
If you take the metal detecting route you ALWAYS clean your coins. Full stop.

Please note that cleaning any coin that has come out of the ground involves unpredictability and risk. You could end up with a coin in worse condition than when you began the cleaning processes. That's because ground conditions vary... Silver quality varies... Hardness / softness of each reader's water supply varies... Purity / strength of the chemicals varies... And any decision about how long you continue a process is a subjective choice and much to do with the eye of the beholder.

All that said ....

Never disregard the advice of the very experienced coin cleaners you will meet at the local detectorists' club. If they say your find is too valuable for a beginner to mess around with, act on what they say. (They will also fill you in very thoroughly on Treasure Trove and other regulations governing seeking and finding with a metal detector). They probably divide their own hammered silver coin finds into three groups:

1. Coins in poor condition, ideal for experimental techniques; expendable if necessary.

2. Coins that look, to the experienced eye, as though they will benefit from cleaning, perhaps revealing an F grade or higher during the process.

3. Coins that look quite unworn beneath any surface dirt and discolouration. If you find two or more in such condition in very close proximity, you may be one of those lucky beginners who stumbles on a hoard.

Let's deal with a few coins in the second group. Wash them thoroughly in warm water to which you have added a few drops of washing-up liquid. A small plastic sandwich box is the ideal container.

Let them soak for half an hour, then remove, dry on a paper towel, inspect. A lot of surface dirt will have floated off, but you may find one or two concretions of tougher cement-like material the washing-up liquid failed to budge. Tackle them with a WOODEN toothpick. Some enthusiasts make their own wooden cleaning sticks by splitting bamboo. I have used the free stirrers given away in coffee shops. Four good cleaning sticks can be made from one stirrer.

Hold the coin very firmly by its edges. Now spit on one of the concretions. The more spit, the better. There are powerful enzymes in human spit that can work wonders as coin cleaners. Stab and jab at the concretion until the stick loses its point. Sometimes the concretion suddenly breaks away from the coin's surface. At other times it gradually turns to a liquid consistency. Wash the coin under running water and inspect. You may wear away several wooden sticks to completely remove a stubborn concretion. Metal in good condition will not mark under the stick; but gritty particles in the concretion could act as abrasives. Don't push them around the coin's surface. Wash them off as they loosen.

If your coin find has what YOU regard as an unsightly grey or black surface obscuring the design, try the following method. Take a small piece of aluminium kitchen foil just big enough to make a parcel around the coin. Don't wrap more than a single layer; and before closing the parcel … yes, it's those enzymes again … spit generously into the parcel, making sure you get spit on both sides of the coin. Close the mini-package and rub it gently between finger and thumb.

If things are working well the aluminium foil should begin to feel quite warm; if things are working very well you should detect a slightly sulphurous smell. Keep rubbing very gently for three or four minutes, then open the package and wash the coin thoroughly under a running tap. Most, perhaps all, of the blackness/greyness should be gone, leaving a silvery but not polished finish.

Heavy coatings of blackness/greyness may remain unaffected by human spit. In that case cut a sheet of aluminium foil just large enough to cover the bottom of that small plastic sandwich box. Sprinkle a generous teaspoonful of washing soda on the aluminium, then place your black/grey coin on the aluminium before pouring in half an inch of boiling water. Allow the water to cool, lift out your coin, wash under running water, then inspect.

Still unhappy? Try the experiment once again, this time using bottled spring water rather than your own tap water, which may be hard and adversely affecting the chemical reactions.

Still unhappy? The last resort must be electrolysis.

WARNING: The electrolysis procedure will produce small amounts of hydrogen and oxygen gasses, which when combined are extremely flammable. The decay of the stainless steel electrode in the solution could add small amounts of chromium to the liquid. Touching the liquid or breathing in the vapour emitted from the liquid should therefore be avoided and the whole process should be carried out only by adults in a well ventilated area. Further information about electrolysis is readily available in libraries and online, and it is recommended that the reader is fully briefed on the hazards of electrolysis before carrying it out! Rotographic can take no responsibility for mis-haps relating to the use of these instructions.

Buy or borrow a six-volt battery charger (Motorcycle owners often have them). Clean out your plastic sandwich box. Then pour in an inch depth of SOFT water. Luckier readers will get soft water straight from the cold tap. The rest of us must either use bottled spring water, or add a small amount of water softener to the plastic box. Next add a level teaspoonful of washing soda to the water and stir until it dissolves. For use as an electrode, grip a stainless steel spoon in the RED/positive crocodile clip. Place the coin to be cleaned in the BLACK/negative crocodile clip so the coin is held by its edges. KEEP THE CLIPS APART. IF THEY TOUCH YOU COULD DAMAGE THE CHARGER.

Wearing rubber gloves, position the coin and the spoon in the water, two inches apart, with the coin face-on to the spoon. Switch on the battery charger. You will at once see bubbles begin to form around the coin. Move the coin closer to the spoon and the bubbling will increase and speed up the cleaning process - but too close will pit the surface. After thirty seconds, AND WITHOUT SWITCHING OFF THE CHARGER, lift the black clip from the water and inspect your coin. If you think it needs more cleaning, lower it into the water and continue the electrolysis treatment for a further fifteen seconds. Again, lift the coin out of the water WITHOUT SWITCHING OFF THE CHARGER.

If the coin now looks much better, SWITCH OFF THE CHARGER, remove the coin from the black crocodile clip, then revert to the spit-and-stick treatment described previously. All surface blackness and concretions should come away very quickly when you wash and dry the coin.

You will see at once that you now have a coin that is nicely cleaned on one side, but still blackened on its other side. Smear the cleaned side with a small amount of Vaseline, then carry out the electrolysis treatment on the second side. It's OK to use the solution still in the plastic box. With obverse and reverse nicely cleaned you must now remove any Vaseline with plenty of washing-up liquid, then allow your coin to dry out fully. Some enthusiasts place coins that have been cleaned by electrolysis into a bath of distilled water for a day to ensure that all traces of chemicals wash from the metal.

With both sides de-greased and cleaned to your satisfaction, you may conclude that the coin looks TOO GOOD TO BE TRUE; that both surfaces are uniformly silver. Perhaps you should have left a little blackness around the lettering of the monarch's head? Fortunately you can reverse the process as follows: Grip the stainless steel spoon in the BLACK/negative crocodile clip. Hold the coin in the RED/positive crocodile clip. Switch on the battery charger BEFORE you lower both clips into the water FOR JUST ONE SECOND. Lift both clips out of the water while the charger is switched on. You should see that blackness has reformed around the lettering. If not, try another one-second dip, again keeping that charger switched on. That should do it.

To Clean Or Not To Clean?

Switch off, wipe the coin dry and examine it. Attractively toned areas should now show around the lettering and designs.

I'll explain the need to keep the battery charger switched on when lifting coins in and out of the liquid. If you leave a coin in the liquid with no current flowing, all of your cleaning efforts will immediately begin to reverse. NEVER leave metal objects in the liquid with the current switched off.

As you will now appreciate, there's as much art as science in those cleaning techniques. That's one good reason for keeping even the poorest grade hammered silver coin find for use as a guinea-pig piece when trying any new cleaning techniques you hear about down at the detectorists' club.

FINALLY ....

I referred to lost farthings at the beginning of this section. There's a strong possibility that you will find lost farthings, as well as lost cut pennies, during your detecting exploits. There are yet unknown varieties of all types of hammered silver coins out there in the ploughsoil. Don't neglect your efforts to learn more about mintmarks, privy marks and rarities. Here are two excellent approaches to knowledge-building:

Use your PC's scanner to make large-scale images of your finds. Build up a database of images for future reference.

Buy the best digital camera you can afford. It MUST have macro facilities that enable you to make close-up images of coins. Take your camera to club meetings. Photograph all hammered silver finds shown at the club by fellow members. Study the images; compile databases; compare with images from dealers' on-line catalogues. Soon - it might take a year, but that's soon enough - you will become quite an expert at identifying English hammered silver coins. When that day comes, this little book will have achieved its objective.....

The Beginning ...

The Cover Images

The main image on the front of this book is of Moneyer Dave Greenhalgh, who is the last remaining proper coin hammerer! He travels the country demonstrating his art and producing little replica and customised hammered coins in various metals. More details on www.grunal.com. The stained glass window and the old parchment are stock images. The knight and his trusty assistant were spotted at Lulworth Castle in Dorset in the summer of 2006. The small coin image shows the obverse of a penny from the reign of Edward the Confessor.

The back cover features another Dorset castle, or at least what's left of it. Corfe Castle is where Edward the Martyr was murdered in 978.